BLIND AMERICANS *on a* GOLDILOCKS PLANET

DAVID J. SLAWSON

BLIND AMERICANS *on a* GOLDILOCKS PLANET

A TRAIL OF DECEPTION PLAYED ON AMERICAN VOTERS

Blind Americans Book
19363 Willamette Drive #186
West Linn, Oregon 97068

ISBNs: 979-8-9909534-0-6 (paperback), 979-8-9909534-1-3 (hardcover), 979-8-9909534-2-0 (ebook)

Cover and book design by Mayfly book design

Library of Congress Catalog Number: 2024912019
First Printing: 2024
Printed in the United States of America

Preface

"The time is always right to do the right thing."

—Martin Luther King Jr.

If you are holding this book in your hand, it is because you are an influencer in American society today. You may be the President of the United States, a former president or a cabinet member, governor, US senator, house member, state legislator, work on Wall Street, the CEO of a big bank, head of a hedge fund or private equity firm or asset management group. You may run an environmental organization, be a CEO in the fossil fuel industry, a journalist or news reporter, a White House correspondent, a podcaster, a radio host, TV host or political commentator, a Hollywood celebrity, music maven, a pastor of a church, minister or priest (all of whom have a duty to warn) a political science educator at a prestigious college or university, in leadership for a minority organization, or a voter, trying to make sense out of the political drama being staged in the media, or someone involved in party politics in the upcoming 2024 November election. This book, "Blind Americans," is for you. It is about politics in America, religion, the state of the planet and public health.

Since knowledge drives decision making, the information provided will be valuable, insightful, and transformative, revealing the underlying causes for America's troubles and divisions. The intent behind this literary endeavor is to influence your decision-making and your communications with the public, but also, provide the solutions to build a better America and export those achievements to the rest of the world.

Author
David J. Slawson

Preface

Contents

Introduction ix

Chapter 1 Blinded by the Sun 1

Chapter 2 The Goldilocks Planet 9

Chapter 3 Space Station 17

Chapter 4 Deadly Fossil Fuel Toxins 21

Chapter 5 Koch Industries Inc 35

Chapter 6 Climate Altering Pollution Sold as a Hoax 43

Chapter 7 Time to Drain the Swamp 53

Chapter 8 Unfit to Serve-Most Destructive President in U.S. History 65

Chapter 9 Maniac Master Mind 85

Chapter 10 Stop the Steal and the Big Lie 91

Chapter 11 Rise of Christian Nationalism 103

Chapter 12 The AntiChrist or Clever Conman 113

Chapter 13 Political Ruse Trickery 123

Chapter 14 Voters Fraud, Voter Suppression & Minority Rule 165

Chapter 15 Voters Guide 175

Chapter 16 Mr. Smith Goes to Washington D.C. 181

Chapter 17 Glossary of Terms 193

Conclusion 205

Introduction

"It's the truth I'm after, and the truth never harmed anyone. What harms us is to persist in self-deceit and ignorance.

—Marcus Aurelius

Picture a political landscape where candidates communicate truths and stand by their words, where their campaign slogans and policy initiatives align unequivocally with their intended purposes, an America built on trust, transparency, and the collective well-being of its citizens.

Reality today deviates from this ideal. Our political stage has become a battleground of conflicting interests. Elected officials, instead of serving the common good, often find themselves entangled in webs of allegiance to special interest groups. In this landscape, voters are forced to be political experts, translators, and vigilant guardians, discerning ingenious acts of deception amid the cacophony of political discourse. The consequence is a population divided, where communities are manipulated out of fear into believing false narratives and individual rights are undermined for the benefit of a select few.

My purpose in writing this book is to unravel the complexities of political deceit, offering readers a lens through which to decipher the subtle art of political trickery. I delve into the manipulative techniques employed by those in power, from carefully crafted slogans to deceptive wordplay. By the book's conclusion, readers will possess tools to identify charlatans and knowledge to discern the truth from political smokescreens. My motivation behind this endeavor is to strip away the blinders that shroud the eyes of American voters to reveal often-hidden truths. Since knowledge drives decision-making, it is important to empower voters to make informed decisions within the democratic system and purge unethical elements from office, thereby fostering a more just society.

The evidence presented in this book is substantial and challenges readers to examine their own beliefs, biases, and the consequences of their actions. I anticipate through this exploration readers may discover their blind spots, prompting a profound change in perspective and voting behavior. The time has come for Americans to be united, transcending political divides, and engage in civil discourse to shape public policies for the greater good. Historically Americans do come together when faced with adversity, such as World War II, the aftermath of 911, and most recently the COVID pandemic, even though certain political and religious leaders shamefully played politics during the COVID crisis, resulting in thousands of unnecessary deaths.

The new challenge facing the public is corporate supremacy with unlimited anonymous money over the people's democracy. Both public and private corporations have joined hands in an allegiance to control the levers of governance, public lands, and the U.S. treasury. They have captured our courts and law-making processes. A conglomerate of the Fortune 500 companies have created the Corporate Political Party which has captured the republican party, yet purposely remains mostly invisible to the public's observations. Voters must become aware of its existence to counteract its power by constraining its tentacles over our government and the national economy.

We can no longer afford to allow ourselves to be pitted, one against another and used by powerful interests, spurred on by false pretenses invoking anger, resentment, and fear, blaming and finger-pointing at the guy who looks different or does not share the same view or religion, has a different sexual orientation or color of skin.

Who is this other guy anyway? He is your neighbor, family member, co-worker, or fellow American. It is important to know you are focusing on the wrong person and thing. Therein lies the fundamental susceptibility for political trickery to work, and why you must be educated to know the difference. Whom you vote for will determine whether you maintain your personal freedoms or come under an authoritarian corporate rule, losing your Social Security, Medicare, Medicaid, Pell Grants, public safety services and more.

Abraham Lincoln at Gettysburg reminded us that "the American destiny is a government of the people, by the people and for the people." We must take to heart this vision and together regain control of our government and its founding principles or we will continue to be ruled by unethical men of power, protecting and expanding their corporate welfare ambitions, who, more than anything else, want to maintain control over the US government for access to public tax revenues and America's natural resources. These forces will not rest until they have domination over all government administrative agencies from the inside enjoying unfettered access to America's entire estate.

These corporations and some multi-nationals, do not care about what is good for America or its 120 million families. If you doubt this, just look at the historical accounts of corporate polluting behavior which has left death and destruction in its wake, or the corporate funded Heritage Foundation's Project 2025 Plan to take over all government agency jobs, filling them with evangelized loyalists. Right now, thousands of individuals are being trained to know how to seize the gears of power effectively. The January 2025 Project Plan calls for readiness on day one of the next Republican Presidency to begin implementing their control over the U.S. government.

One quarter of Americans cannot name the three branches of government, and most have no civic education. These Americans can easily be deceived by political lip service while their rights are being subverted and terrible things are done in their name. They are oblivious to the fact their elected officials are working for corporate monied interests and not theirs. Elected officials have even signed Koch Industry loyalty pledges, against their oath of office, to corporate interests that are antithetical to the public good. This sleight of hand political trickery is cunning, clever, and deceptive with effective ad buys numbering in the hundreds of thousands. The average voter cannot see what is going to happen because their intent is never to reveal the truth, always stick with the lie, as it is the foundational operating principle of deception. Never disclose who is behind the campaign ad. It is the only way their political gamesmanship can continue to work. It is difficult to grasp the in-your-face culture war language, religious doctrine bias or other made-up conservative wedge issues that purposely become "the distraction,"

Slogans such as *compassionate conservatism, clear sky initiative, healthy forests, no child left behind, religious freedom is under attack, evil leftist democrats, climate change is a hoax, America first agenda, make America great again, right to work state, two-tiered justice system, weaponized FBI, Trump is not an insurrectionist, media is the enemy* are all a political ruse to give you a false impression of something good or bad for American citizenry. I have devoted an entire chapter deciphering dozens of slogans and word smithing techniques. By reviewing these examples, you will gain insight, enabling you to identify deception in action. It will be empowering when you possess the knowledge and tools to recognize when you are being played. It will be liberating when you are able to see through the fog of politics, know the truth and vote accordingly.

By the end of this book, I want the reader to know, to see and understand you have the power to "drain the swamp." I list the names of 167 deemed unethical politicians who must be voted out of office. The reason is they are controlled by corporate money. Their cowardly actions and inability to do their job defending your rights is cause for removal from office. This will require independent voters, the largest bloc of voters, to take the lead with democrats and republicans ousting individuals within their own parties, and then imposing ethical standards for new perspective candidates for office to buck corporate power in favor of the people's agenda. In this book, I provide a voter's guide, listing public policies a candidate should support before receiving your vote.

An informed voter can obliterate the lies and deceit being perpetrated on the American citizens, lies that trespass on individuals' rights and personal freedoms, lies designed to erase one's memory about history, about real events that happened. Certain people do not want you to remember. For example, claiming the terrorist attack on our capital was a group of tourist and the January 6th's subversion, violent actions are being portrayed as patriots expressing their grievances. Those imprisoned for their acts of violence are "patriots" being held hostage. Certain members of Congress are perpetuating this deceitfulness because they are bound together in a collective communication framing based on lies. By cherry picking statements and perpetuating the lies, they are trying to make the truth imperceptible to the public so they can keep the "us versus them" mentality to beat their opponents. My intent is to create an awakening for American voters, jolting them out of their stupor to remove their blinders and bring out the best in the American people by appealing to our better nature.

I am reaching out to all voters whether you are a conservative republican, MAGA republican, democrat, independent, and the mix of rural voters who love their country and who are patriotic and committed to protecting everyone's inalienable rights and our democratic form of government. Today there is a deep divide between Americans. One group, the republicans are purposely creating chaos to set the stage for an authoritarian strong man, and changing election laws in Republican-controlled swing states to commandeer electors for their preferred candidate. The goal is to gain the White House with enhanced presidential powers fused with corporate interests.

The other group, the democrats are advancing democracy of the people, by the people and for the people with enhanced individual rights, such as the right to vote, the right to choose whom to love, equality among all races, women's control over their own bodies, clean food, air, and water. My goal is to bridge the divide by shedding light on the shared values we all have in common and uniting Americans around a common purpose to diminish corporate power in favor of the people's government.

"Blind Americans on a Goldilocks Planet" has been written to provide insight into the power structure in American politics, religious beliefs, the state of our "Goldilocks Planet," and public health. I am writing from the perspective of an independent voice bearing witness to an assault on our constitution. Since this is election year 2024, a lot of political theater and drama is being played out in the public sphere. I must bring to light the destructive nature of one of the most powerful authoritarian strong men in American politics today, Donald J. Trump. This is the time; this is the hour to sound the alarm. I am calling upon every voter, elected official, corporate stakeholder, religious leader, and the media to have the moral courage to speak out against Trump's authoritarian, retribution agenda, condemning his rhetoric and making it clear that he cannot be trusted to hold the reins of power. You must stand on the side of democracy and decency and loudly speak out against his reelection.

It is my hope that the information in these pages will alter personally held beliefs. After all, a belief is only a thought that one keeps thinking. My objective is to follow the truth and share with the reader what I have found to be true. I encourage every MAGA voter to take the time to watch and listen to the January 6th hearings with an open mind. This investigative committee documents Trump's words and actions leading up to and on January 6th. You will hear from Trump lawyers, his Attorney General Bill Barr, Ivanka Trump, and White House staffers who were all hired by Trump. You will learn what Trump knew, what he did and why over 1,400 individuals were charged with crimes related to January 6th. It is laid out in an easy-to-follow format.

Also watch Biden's State of the Union Address from March 7, 2024. See firsthand how the republican party is purposely blocking a bipartisan conservative immigration border fix. Instead of fixing the problem the intent is to use the border crisis as a political wedge issue. Republicans are abandoning the need for public safety and national security. An informed and educated citizenry is what is required to understand who the bad actors are, who is funding them and why. To protect our democratic form of government, voters must see through the veil of deception to recognize the truth—like seeing a solar eclipse for the first time.

Warning! This book is intended to elicit emotion, to amuse, to anger, to inspire and in the end to advance American society by challenging established ideas, recognizing that truths, no matter how inconvenient, undergo a transformative journey—from ridicule to vehement opposition—before acceptance is self-evident.

CHAPTER 1

Blinded by the Sun

"Eternal vigilance is the price of Liberty; power is ever stealing from the many to the few."

—Thomas Jefferson

Democracy requires participation and citizens educated about current events. It requires being a savvy consumer of media information and paying attention to what is going on behind the scenes. Voters have been blindsided by a relentless bombardment of manufactured panic, fear, resentment, and looney lies. Conjured up by well financed think tanks, the propaganda has been so effective some voters no longer get information from reputable journalistic sources, convinced they create fake news and that traditional media is the enemy of the people. Social media has created silos of discontent, conspiracy theories, and false information in a closed person to person feedback loop, reinforcing personally held false beliefs that the other side are leftist evil doers, socialists-soon-to-become communists and liberals are out to negate conservative values, wanting to make conservatives into second class citizens. The only good guys are the "R" candidates. It is no wonder Americans are blind to the truth with all the false propaganda and political ruses. It is like driving toward the horizon and being blinded by the sun.

Who are the blind Americans who have eyes yet cannot see? Are you blind to something? Do you have blind faith in something? Do you ignore something that is shady, immoral, or illegal? Do you pretend not to notice something happening, so you do not have to do anything about it? How is it truth can go unnoticed? What activities are going on behind a constructed veil of deception? Are Americans knowingly out to destroy America? Are Americans in pursuit of winning elections to maintain power knowingly or naively destroying the very fabric of American democracy? Are your actions and beliefs helping to strengthen the tenets of America democracy or undermining it? Are you blind to the suffering and marginalization of certain members of society? Do you lack empathy? Are you blinded by personal greed? Are you indifferent to the less fortunate amongst us? Are you ignoring the truth or unaware of it? Why does a person's beliefs cause people to behave in unreasonable, even in violent ways? Why do people defend the indefensible? Are you close-minded and unable to hear the truth? Are you living in fear or driven by it? What is true for you?

John Pilger, journalist and co-writer of the documentary "How the Government Manipulates Facts," profiles Edward Bernays, who invented the term "public relations." He wrote, "The intelligent manipulation of the masses is an invisible government, which is the true ruling power in our country." He was part of a secretive group called the US Committee on Public Information, set up in 1917 to persuade reluctant Americans to join the war in Europe. Edward Bernays went to Woodrow Wilson and said, "If you're going to enter this war, we are going to need to sell this war to the American people." And so, Wilson instituted and created the first modern propaganda machinery. It was quite brilliant in its conceptualization, as Edward Bernays said, the "best way to persuade people is to grab them by their emotions, by their unconscious and instinctual urges. Let us not bother with pumping out facts. Let us scare the hell out of people."

This is exactly what George Bush and Dick Cheney did in their march to war in Iraq. First, they convinced the public there was a link between Sadam Hussein's regime and 911. Then, using propaganda, convinced the American public that Sadam Hussein had weapons of mass destruction. They used Secretary of State Colin Powell to peddle similar lies to the United Nations and all media outlets. In the end they got their war to remove Sadam Hussein from power. But their war killed between 946,000 and 1,120,000 Iraqi citizens, displaced 4.5 million Iraqis from their homes, leaving 750,000 woman and children without a husband and father, and in effect, making the United States the enemy.

According to the U.S. Defense Department 4,431 U.S. soldiers were killed in action and another 31,994 were wounded. Since 911, the number of military service members who committed suicide is over 30,177 stemming from psychological wounds such as PTSD. According to Joseph Stiglitz, former chief economists at the World Bank and Nobel Prize winner in economics, and Linda Blimes, a Harvard University professor the cost of the Iraq war on the U.S. economy was $3 trillion dollars. Not the two year $100 billion estimate that Dick Cheney stated in his interview with Tim Russert prior to the war. The Iraq war did enrich the military industrial complex of weapons companies and service contractors like Halliburton.

The democratic principles of equality and personal freedoms have never been more important. Today our democracy is under attack from an enemy within. Through a combination of money and power ambitions, ignorance, and a self-righteous religious agenda, our self-governing way of life is teetering on the abyss, dominated by elected officials who are hell-bent on forcing an authoritarian, religious dictatorial and corporate rule over America. This is happening because millions of voters do not understand how democracy works and are confused and overwhelmed by pungent opinions and thousands of disinformation advertisements peddled by corporate ownership of the media and billions spent on propaganda from corporate think tanks.

American voters are unwittingly ready to throw it all away by relinquishing their personal responsibilities for a figure who found in voters an effective emotional hook to manipulate them, based on past grievances, victimhood, and fear. They have become mentally entrapped in a psychological inner group collective, fixated on their impenetrably held beliefs that are unchallengeable, even in the face of overwhelming evidence to the contrary.

Voters have been convinced to fear the Muslims living next door, that biased ideas about LGBTQ+ individuals are justified by interpretations rooted in religious text, myths, and fear. People of color and non-English speaking people have become piñatas in the race to the White House.

Evangelical Christians believe our founding fathers founded this nation to be Christian and therefore it belongs to Christians only. Ambitious politicians pander to Evangelicals to garner votes from this large voting bloc, claiming their beliefs must be imposed on the nation to prevent further social decay. Separation of church and state is guaranteed by the First Amendment: "Congress shall make no law respecting an establishment of religion." The separation of church and state ensures the government cannot exercise undue influence over Americas' spiritual and religious lives. The Founders never intended to create a society where all are forced to worship the God of a particular religion. This would be particularly problematic since today there are over 370 established religions in America, each believing they have the one true God and set of beliefs.

Regardless of religious or political party affiliation all Americans want their individual freedoms protected, such as freedom of movement, freedom of religious worship, freedom to decide whom they want to love. They want control over their own bodies and to make their own healthcare decisions. Responsible citizens have the right to bear arms, but at the same time want to be protected from criminals and disturbed people owning weapons. Americans want pollution eradicated so they can breathe clean air, have access to clean water and safe food to eat, and they want cancer-causing chemicals ravaging Americans stopped.

Americans want a flourishing natural environment in which to live, and pollution abated to prevent mega storms, the kind that destroy homes, take lives, and wipe out a community's infrastructure. In the past 30 years over fourteen million Americans have experienced the loss of life and property they worked a lifetime to build.

If you use the power of your vote and choose your elected official wisely you can determine your quality-of-life outcomes and solve an array of pressing problems affecting all Americans equally. It is important to listen critically to the words of politicians. Their words matter as they reveal the nature of their character, as well as disclose if they are corporately owned or serving the public's interest. Politicians use wedge issues to manipulate you, instead of supporting policies to make life better for everyone.

Some examples are calls to end Woke-ism, Critical Race Theory (CRT), and the deep state, as well as statements and catch phrases like "The government is the problem," "burdensome government overregulation," "the weaponization of the Justice Department," "Get rid of the EPA and IRS, masks and vaccine mandates," "Crime is rampant," "fake news," "Climate change is a hoax," "Demonize LGBTQ+ rights," "Ban the books," "parental rights and transparency in the classroom," "evil democrats," "war on coal," "war on American energy," "Democrats are leftist, socialist, communist, pedophiles," "Democrats are destroying America," "race baiting," "tax and spend liberals," "culture wars," "cancel culture," "political correctness," "replacement theory," "Deregulation is needed to unleash economic growth," "energy independence-drill baby drill," "Renewables are costly, not reliable and won't solve our energy problem," "Electric vehicles are expensive and not dependable," "The democrats want to take your guns, your hamburgers, your gas stoves, your light bulbs, and your bibles," "Democratic ideology is responsible for the crime and social decay in our society".

Be an independent critical thinker and do not fall for divisive, deceitful political ruses and give your vote away stupidly. Otherwise, you'll end up with laws and policies antithetical to your family's wellbeing and enable our national government and its public service agencies to be under corporate control. For example, voter choices have allowed the highest court in the land, the "Supreme Court," to become a partisan policy court eroding public safety, democratic values and giving polluters a free pass. The principal code in voting must be for the best candidate regardless of political party affiliation. You must see beyond the negative demonization, and lying ads. Your vote must dictate good public policy where the elected official is to steward those policies into law, not the policies wanted by corporate election campaign contributors.

Your vote smartly used would solve crime, public safety matters, immigration, national security concerns, food and water safety, climate altering pollution, lower of the cost of living, improve education, lower childcare costs and unemployment, improve cyber security, set AI controls, protect individual freedoms, further gun policies that prevent domestic violence and mass shootings, and put an end to high insurance costs, the lack of affordable housing, income inequality, social media's negative attributes, CIA clandestine operations, failed foreign policies, and more.

Yes, these problems are all solvable based on who you vote for and the policies they adhere to. Make your elected official agree to policies to solve these issues in order to secure your vote and financial support. How do you sort out these issues and produce a unified policy agenda? The first thing is to understand what the underlying truth is related to these complex matters. Do not succumb to the influence of political jargon around wedge issues and fear designed to divide, fragment, and detract an otherwise powerful public voting bloc.

It is time to turn the tables and change the political game in the people's favor. Know what you want and impose conditions on politicians to gain your vote. There are certain values most Americans hold in common and do agree on. Americans want to feel safe in their own homes. Americans want the freedom to go about their days without having to worry about their or their family's safety, whether going to work, in church, at the park, shopping for groceries, at a night club, movie theater or just out for an evening stroll in their neighborhood.

John Adams stated, *"There is a danger from all men. The only maxim of a free government ought to be to trust no man living with power to endanger the public liberty."*

Demand transparency and make sure every action in government serves the common good. Not just wealthy individuals and corporations advancing their corporate agendas, along with their modus operandi of opposing all regulatory oversight which interferes in any way with their free market indifference to public health and safety.

CHAPTER 2

The Goldilocks Planet

"Man's attitude toward nature is today critically important simply because we have now acquired a fateful power to alter and destroy nature. But man is part of nature, and his war against nature is inevitably a war against himself."

—Rachel Carson

According to radiometric rock dating the earth is 4.54 billion years old. When the earth was one hundred million years old, an object the size of Mars crashed into the earth slinging magma out into earth's orbit. Eventually gravitational forces formed planet earth. The earth is in the "Goldilocks" zone. Due to the earth's location in our solar system and proximity to the sun, it is not too hot, nor too cold, exactly the right climate for life to exist. Complex life forms began to appear on earth 2.5 million years ago. Humans evolved from these lower life forms. Estimates suggest that 117 billion members of our species have been born on Earth.

The Goldilocks story began over 13.8 billion years ago when an incomprehensible concentration of heat, energy and matter exploded. This explosion distributed matter and energy across a vast expanse of empty space, spreading hot gaseous material, combining particles, protons, electrons, and neutrons and causing billions and trillions of stars, planets, and galaxies to form. There are around

200 sextillion stars in the universe. This event is known as the "Big Bang" cosmology, accidentally discovered by two American radio astronomers Arno Penzias and Robert Wilson and earning them a Nobel Prize in physics. They uncovered electromagnetic radiation known as the "relic radiation." Cosmic microwave background radiation (CMBR) is the remnant from the early stage of the universe. This is the evidence of the "Big Bang" origin of the universe.

The earth is one of nine planets in our solar system orbiting the Sun. The earth is the third planet from the sun with a circumference of 24,901 miles. The earth spins at 1,000 miles per hour. Earth's orbital speed around the sun is 67,000 miles per hour completing a single orbit in 365 days. The size of our sun is equivalent to 1.3 million earths. UY Scuti is the largest red hyper giant sun in the Milky Way. Located 9,500 light years from earth, UY Scuti's mean radius is 432,450 miles around and equivalent to 5 billion of our suns. If UY Scuti were the center of our universe its photosphere would reach just past the orbit of Jupiter. The celestial planets in our solar system are millions and billions of miles from our sun. Closest planet to the sun is Mercury at 32.54 million miles away, the most heavily cratered object in our solar system, a dead planet with little gravity to hold an atmosphere. Venus is 66.77 million miles away from the sun. Once considered an earth twin due to its matching size, Venus is 24.80 million miles from earth. A runaway volcanic greenhouse effect turned Venus into hell. Earth is 91.57 million miles away from our sun, Mars is 140.31 million miles, Jupiter is 463.78 million miles, Saturn is 920.07 million miles, Uranus is 1.832 billion miles, Neptune is 2.780 billion miles, and Pluto is 3.202 billion miles away. In another 4.5 billion years our sun will expand into a giant red Supernova event, creating a fiery hydrogen explosion consuming the earth.

The diameter of the observable universe is believed to be ninety-three billion light years. The unobservable universe is estimated to be over 7 trillion light years across. A single light year is equivalent to six trillion miles. Our solar system is located inside the Kuiper belt that lies beyond the orbit of Neptune, toward the outer edge of the Milky Way galaxy. Our Milky Way galaxy is 105,700 light years across. Traveling at the speed of light it would take 200,000 years for a spaceship to cross the Milky Way galaxy. The Andromeda Galaxy (M31), the closest spiral galaxy, is 2.4 trillion light years away.

The closest potentially habitable Goldilocks planet to earth is Proxima Centauri b in the Milky Way. Its distance from earth is 4.2 light years (25.2 trillion miles) away. A spacecraft traveling at a speed of light would take 17,157 years to reach Proxima Centauri b. To put this into perspective, NASA's Voyager II satellite has been traveling in space at 36,000 miles per hour for the past 44 years. By the time the battery runs out in 2024, Voyager II will have only traveled about thirteen billion miles. Or faster still is the Parker Solar Probe—top speed 430,000 miles per hour, so fast it can travel the circumference of the earth in 4.5 seconds or fly from the earth to the moon round trip in about 40 minutes. Yet this is only 0.064% of the speed of light.

The earth has a hot molten inner iron core with an electromagnetic field that shields and reflects immense solar radiation, enabling life to exist. A layer of soil about thirty-nine inches deep sustains all life. An atmosphere of oxygen and nitrogen enables us to breathe. The earth is a fragile biosphere perfectly calibrated to support life.

Recently man's negative influence has altered the natural forces, putting our planet in peril and jeopardizing our very existence. Ecological collapse is no longer a prediction but a real and present danger that cannot be denied. The burning of fossil fuel by human activity is the culprit. The "force" changing our climate today. It is imperative that every American recognize the precarious reality in which we live and the necessity to stop burning fossil fuels.

Every person alive today will die, just like all the emperors, presidents, tycoons, soldiers, laborers, and religious believers before us.

The Earth is a place where thousands of gods and kings have come and gone. The thinking mind can be a trickster, lulling man to think he is fully awake and conscious. But this is not true. Of this, I am certain. The evidence is all around us. If man were fully awake, fully conscious of the cosmos he would not play God and judge others. People would not be killing one another over a personal point of view, fits of rage, nationalism, territorial confiscation, ethnic difference, racial discrimination, religious beliefs or creeds, gender stuff, one God's superiority, or political ideologies.

A fully conscious person would recognize that we are the same. I am you and you are me, all the same. What you do to others harms everyone including you. Until man comes to terms with his ill treatment of his fellow human beings, recognizes his existence as being part of nature and the impermanence of his existence, he will continue to sleepwalk, mesmerized by entertainment, talking heads, technologies, unfolding world events, personal prejudice, beliefs, and greed, all the while dismissive of information that challenges one's beliefs. Man has become unresponsive to his pending fate. It is as if he is numb, unable to comprehend the grandeur of the cosmos and natural world in which he lives. He blindly extracts natures capital in a destructive fashion taking what he can, destroying forest, using the atmosphere as a sewer, and polluting the land and water ways that nourish us. We have a choice. Continue wrecking the planet and doom humanity or live in harmony with nature and one another. We can build stronger economies, have better health outcomes and security when we preserve and restore the Goldilocks planet.

It is important for individuals to understand what must be done to restore our Goldilocks planet. Smart individual actions can create the political and economic changes needed to have a fully functioning democracy and solve the pollution-altering climate crisis. The level of environmental degradation by human activity is accelerating at an alarming rate. Evidence demonstrates that we have exceeded the sustainability of the planet by 25%. What does this mean? It means we exceeded the constraint of natural forces in nature that support our life by a combination of human-induced carbon emissions warming the planet, deforestation, and land-use changes. Recently, Antarctica has warmed by 3.5 degrees, reaching a temperature of 70 degrees, like California. Across the world massive forest fires have destroyed vast wilderness areas in the millions of acres and caused the death of countless wildlife. Massive flash flooding has taken place on every continent causing death, destruction, and homelessness. Twenty thousand cold snap records and forty thousand elevated temperature records have been surpassed, heading to extreme degrees of warming, creating an uninhabitable planet.

Extreme weather events require new terminology to describe nature's fury. Excess carbon has weaponized nature, hitting us with consecutive mega storms, rain bombs, sky rivers, atmospheric rivers, flash flooding, cyclone bombs, snow bursts, polar vortex, baseball size hailstorms, heat waves, heat blobs, heat domes, extended droughts, and fire tornados. We have exponentially gone from 280 Parts Per Million (PPM) of carbon to over 421 PPM in less than 70 years with the greatest change in the last 30 years. This CO2 is trapped in the earths' atmosphere and is measurable. As such we have caused large scale planetary shifts in our natural environment, including a 2% oxygen level deficit in the air we breathe, the melting of Arctic Sea ice and changing jet stream patterns, ocean current temperatures and seasonal weather. We have created heat waves in Siberia, destabilizing methane hydrates, increasing ocean acidity and causing fish to struggle to survive. Sulfuric acid droplets are in our atmosphere and our cities are polluted with toxic molecules.

Half of the Great Barrier Reef of Australia has died off. In 2020 Australian bushfires burned 46 million acres (72,000 square miles), destroyed 3,500 homes, killed 34 people, and killed over 3 billion animals. Ocean circulation is changing and oceans are awash with disposable plastics, killing marine life and contaminating the food chain with lethal effects to humans. Biodiversity of life in parts of the world is being destroyed. Today, rising sea levels due to rapid melting of our glaciers is putting $67 trillion dollars of US real estate assets at risk of being inundated with water. In the last four years over one hundred million climate refugees were forcibly on the move, eating powdered meals to survive. Underscoring what is yet to come.

"The earth mourns and withers; the world languishes and fades; the exalted of the earth wastes away. The earth is defiled by its people, they have transgressed the laws; they have overstepped the decrees and broken the everlasting covenant." (Isaiah Chapter 24.) For the first time, we are forced to consider the real risks of destabilizing the entire planet as all-natural systems are intrinsically linked.

We as a nation have had a flaw in our thinking continued from one generation to the next. That is the false premise of extracting eco systems for profits. It is this kind of thinking which has led us to our current predicament of collapsing fragile ecosystems, when the highest productive values come from preserving eco systems as a source of abundance and regeneration. It is time to restore our biological life forms for our own survival's sake. One of the best ways is regenerative ocean agriculture and regenerative farming practices, building up soil and pulling carbon out of the atmosphere. Eighty-seven percent of life forms on this planet – microbes, worms, insects, birds, animals, human beings, plants, trees, and every other vegetation – is sustained by three feet of topsoil. And that is in grave danger right now.

In the last forty years, forty percent of the world's topsoil has been lost. The United Nations stated we have only enough soil left for eighty to one hundred harvests, which means another forty-five to sixty years of agriculture. After that, we will not have the soil to produce food. You can imagine the suffering that we will unfold in the world. We can no longer stand by and allow productive farmlands to turn to desert. Our future actions must ensure our planet is recognizable and inhabitable in the coming decades.

Man-induced climate change can only be fixed by retooling our society with options that do not destroy our natural environment while sustaining our lives. Solving these problems will involve every citizen, legislature, corporation, financial market, small business, and government agency. It will affect job options, what we buy, how we source and use energy and how we treat one another.

CHAPTER 3

Space Station

"Throw your dreams into space like a kite, and you do not know what it will bring back, a new life, a new friend, a new love, a new country."

—Anais Nin.

The international space station (ISS) is an engineering marvel. It took 10 years and thirty missions carrying payloads of construction materials. The ISS is about the size of a football field including the end zones. The ISS gets its power supply from an acre size photovoltaic solar panel array and utilizes two propulsion systems—a gaseous H/O rockets for high thrust applications and the multi-propellant "resist jets" for low thrust—to maintain orbit and avoid space debris. The ISS has sleeping quarters, two toilets and a gym. It cost $150 billion to construct. The ISS is in an orbit 254 miles above the earth traveling at 17,500 miles per hour, circumventing the earth every ninety-two minutes. Astronauts can witness sixteen dawns per day as they pass over the terminator line, the line between light and darkness.

Imagine for a moment that your wife entered your name in a nationwide lottery to travel to the ISS. You were always boasting about how you wanted to be an astronaut, but your life just did not work out that way. You pull into your driveway and a crowd has gathered to congratulate you as you walk to the front door. Your boss gives you the time off with pay. On the following Monday you are off to NASA for twelve weeks of training. You must get in shape. Lose weight and build muscle mass. You are told to get off the "Standard American Diet" (SAD), avoid sugars, particularly high-fructose corn syrup, wheat, soy, and cut back on red meat and stop eating nutrition-less processed foods and avoid food additives. Instead, eat healing whole foods consisting of fruits, vegetables, nuts, seeds, whole grains, beans, super foods, and limit animal protein. You're offered "Moringa Leaf Powder" to drink daily to lose weight and reduce inflammation. Following the fitness and nutritionist program you gain more muscle mass and strength. You feel great, full of energy, have more flexibility and mental clarity.

You are now physically and mentally ready on launch day. Strapped in a bucket seat on top of a giant multi-stage rocket over three hundred feet in the air, you are ready to be projected into space. The countdown begins, then lift off. You can hear the roar of the rocket busters and feel the shaking from propulsion burning 15,000 gallons of fuel every second. You struggle to deal with 7x G Force against your body. Nine minutes and a few seconds later you pop into space orbit. One day later you catch up with the space station. You begin docking at the Quest Joint Airlock port. Guided by the radar transponder you come within inches of the airlock docking port. You exit the space capsule into the double doored airlock compartment. You move slowly to avoid decompression sickness as pressurization takes place. Entering the harmony capsule you begin to float where you will be living for the next six months. The astronauts on board remind you not to "fart" as the smell can linger due to the lack of circulation. You are told a "fart" is like a ticking time bomb. . .the gases are flammable with nowhere to go. Methane is a particularly volatile gas in a closed environment. So, use the suction toilet. You quickly adapt learning how to use the suction toilet and sleep tethered onto a wall-mounted bunk. Soon you become used to the constant hum of the space station.

Your greatest enjoyment is in Cupola at the bottom of the space station with its 360-degree view of the Goldilocks Planet. From this point of view hovering above you become awestruck with the majestic blue marble-like beauty of earth. Effortlessly floating in space, you are alone in the Cupola, missing your wife and kids. Soon you feel overwhelmed with emotion. You begin to weep, then cry uncontrollably overcome by a deep sense of love. You think about your life on earth. For the first time in your life, you see yourself, your habits, and interactions with others like an out of body experience looking down on yourself, or watching yourself in a movie acting out your life. You come face to face with your prejudices, pettiness, and false beliefs.

As you circumvent the earth you become acutely aware of the ecological degradation done at the hands of man. The forest fires, desertification, and land mass changes. You reflect on seeing no borders. Knowing war is taking place in Ukraine and the Middle East out of fear, religious beliefs, and land disputes. A feeling of peace sweeps over your body. You enter a state of heightened consciousness as if a veil had been removed. Like the clouds passing revealing a bright sunny day or the moon eclipsing the sun. You become aware, awake, knowing how to live your life more joyfully. You make a pledge to yourself to live more consciously and be part of the solution to save the planet. You decide to quit your coal job for one in the renewable energy industry, trade in your gasoline powered truck for an all-electric one. You have an urge to commune with nature, walk barefoot in the grass, dig in the dirt, start a garden, and plant fruit trees in your back yard.

The next day fellow astronaut Max joins you in the Copula. He points out 2,000 square miles of broken up great barrier islands around Louisiana, caused by oil and gas development, leaving the area vulnerable to storm surges and flooding. A short while later you're observing Africa's Great Green Wall, a tree barrier running 5,000 miles across the continent to hold back the Sahara Desert, although not complete. Soon the Great Green Wall in China is visible. Stretching 3,000 miles in length and nine hundred miles wide, planted to hold back the Gobi Desert now within 150 miles of

Beijing. Max tells you that two billion trees are planted every year, and about the people of Ethiopia setting a record planting 350 million tree saplings in 12 hours. You feel hopeful for humanity.

On your last day before the decent module docks to take you back to the Goldilocks Planet you are in the Copula. Next to you is Abby telling you to look out in the direction of 9 o'clock. Do you see that massive ice shelf? It is the Eastern Siberian Arctic Ice Shelf. It acts as an impermeable lid preventing methane gas from escaping. Scientists warned nations, due to excessive warming of the planet this permafrost could melt. If it does, this ticking fifty gigaton methane bomb would escape into the atmosphere. Pushing global temperatures into double digits over safe limits, making our goldilocks planet mostly uninhabitable.

We have doubled the amount of carbon into the atmosphere in the last 30 years. We are on an exponential growth curve. The human mind is not equipped to think in terms of exponential factors. Professor Chris Martenson gives a splendid example to help understand exponential factors. Suppose you are at Fenway Park and the stadium has been made watertight. The time is 12 noon. You are handcuffed to the top row of bleachers. On the pitcher's mound you see a person with an eye dropper of water. Starting with the first drop, the amount of water doubles every minute. After 6 minutes you have a thimble full of water. How long do you have to get out of your handcuffs before you drown? In just 49 minutes, Fenway Park will be filled with water and you, my friend, will have drowned. What is amazing is the stadium is 93% empty at 12:44 with just five feet of water. I get it. The action really heats up in the last moments. I would drown in five minutes, not realizing the severity of my predicament. That is right, and the carbon impact is on an exponential growth curve. What is coming at us is hard for the human brain to comprehend. The fault, dear Brutus, is not in the stars, but in ourselves.

CHAPTER 4

Deadly Fossil Fuel Toxins

"The right of the public to the nation's natural resources outweigh private rights" His precept: "The nation behaves well if it treats the natural resources as assets which it must turn over to the next generation increased, and not impaired, in value."

—Teddy Roosevelt

Fossil fuels have been the economic engine which built America's modern cities, transportation infrastructure, our agriculture industry, enabled us to defeat the Nazis in World War II and so much more. It is important that we acknowledge with gratitude those innovators, oil wildcatters, and coal miners who spent a lifetime providing energy to America, remembering all those who gave their lives fueling our modern society, including those still working in the industry today.

However, we cannot let the fossil fuel industry dictate the future of the world. Some fossil fuel CEOs have purposefully lied or paid others to lie, misleading the public and its shareholders about the deadly effects from burning fossil fuels.

For decades, their deception and cover up prevented the public and school children from learning the truth about climate change and its societal costs. These titans of great wealth corruptly infiltrated government agencies, the US Senate, House of Representatives and state legislatures. Too many of our elected officials enabled and perpetuated their deceitful activity. These congressional backers aided the taking of our natural resources from the American commonwealth for pennies on the dollar, while avoiding environmental regulatory oversight. It is time for the fossil fuel industry giants to stop their climate altering pollution.

Oil, coal, and natural gas are non-renewable finite resources formed when prehistoric plants, algae, bacteria, and animals died and were gradually buried by layers of rock, dating back to the Devonian Period 419.2 million years ago. As with any finite non-renewable energy resource it will run out. Since 1980 the world has consumed forty trillion gallons of gas. The world has consumed in the past fifty years more than 1.306 trillion barrels of oil. The United States consumes 123 billion gallons of gas per year. That is 338 million gallons per day, and 2.7 million gallons a minute. The world consumes 92.2 million barrels per day. According to World Oil Statistics information, global oil reserves of 1.7 trillion barrels will be exhausted in 47 years at current rate of consumption. According to the U.S. Energy Administration, the United States will be out of oil by 2052 just 28 years from now. Which is another reason we must stop burning our oil. We need it as lubricating oil, for various plastics, and a wide variety of consumer goods. The United States has 86 years of natural gas left and 435 years of coal left. Excluding unproven fossil fuel reserves which, if found, may be uneconomical to produce. Natural gas is a cleaner fuel now being used in the transition to the newly emerging clean energy economy.

The fingerprint of fossil fuel burning emissions matches the rise in global temperature, verifiable by measuring the amount of carbon thirteen and excess carbon in the atmosphere. Current excess carbon above the natural absorption rates by land masses and oceans is 30 Gigatons (GT). For the past 800,000 years parts per million (ppm) of carbon were between 180 to 280 ppm. Now it is above 421ppm. The excess carbon added to the atmosphere each year is 15 GT or (2 ppm). Excess carbon in the atmosphere increases the amount of water molecules due to the warming effect, driving more severe weather events across the planet. Current climate warming models do agree with observation and sophisticated measurements. No doubt about it, burning fossil fuels is the smoking gun. The sooner we phase out fossil fuels the cheaper it will be for everyone.

Coal plants produce airborne cancer-causing toxins including mercury, arsenic, and lead. Coal burning releases nitrogen oxides (NOx) and sulfur dioxide (SO2) which, when combined, cause a chemical reaction producing acid rain. These toxins along with particulates contribute to smog, haze, respiratory illnesses, and lung disease. Coal fired plants are the largest source of mercury pollution in the United States, emitting 8,800 pounds annually (Global Energy Monitor Wiki). Coal is hazardous every step of the way. From mining, transporting, combustion and disposal. Coal washing uses millions of gallons of our aquifer clean drinking water.

The mining process produces solid mining refuse and liquid coal waste. Coal combustion produces coal ash and flue gas solid waste residue. Coal ash contains massive quantities of mercury and other toxic metals, as well as thousands of tons of arsenic, beryllium, cadmium, hexavalent chromium, nickel, and selenium. Millions of tons of coal ash have been produced. Coal waste is more radioactive than nuclear waste. Coal ash contains concentration levels of Uranium and Thorium which can leach into surrounding groundwater and soil.

Robert Finkelman, a former US Geological researcher estimates, "for people living around coal plants, exposure will increase by 5% every year." According to a report released by Earthjustice and the Sierra Club in February, 2011, cancer-causing chemicals are found at 29 sites in seventeen states. They are Arkansas, Delaware, Florida, Illinois, Indiana, Minnesota, Massachusetts, North Carolina, North Dakota, Nevada, Ohio, Oklahoma, Pennsylvania, Tennessee, Virginia, West Virginia, and Wisconsin.

Coal ash-waste and waste landfills are held in lined surface impoundments. According to an EPA study most liners decay over time. A 10-acre landfill will leak up to ten gallons per day, or 36,000 gallons over a ten-year period, which are guaranteed to leak toxins into streams and drinking water supplies. (Feb.24, 2010 Environmental Integrity Project and Earthjustice report).

Coal burning causes low birth weight and preterm births, neurological and development damage in humans and animals, impairs cognitive learning, causes a host of respiratory illnesses and early death. Mercury is ubiquitous in our soil and in the fish we eat. Less than a 1/4 teaspoon of mercury can pollute a twenty-five acre lake. According to a 2011 Harvard report, "Mining Coal, Mounting Coal Costs, the Life Cycle Consequences of Coal," the external costs of coal burning, mining, processing, and transporting are more than $500 billion annually.

By adopting a new national energy efficiency standard for cities, homes, and businesses where coal-derived electricity is used, the demand for coal can be eliminated. Homeowners would participate in a home energy efficiency retrofit program, designed to replace inefficient doors, windows, heaters, boilers, and appliances and add weather stripping and insulation. As well as roof top solar with battery storage. All could be paid for from the savings from not burning coal. Homeowners would be living in more comfortable homes with appreciated value. This would boost American manufacturing and construction employment. Coal workers in the coal industry would have better jobs in a clean economy. Today workers are pitted against their family's health and wellbeing for a paycheck. For far too long the coal industry has benefited from their powerful lobbyists keeping coal alive and buying off legislators to protect their menace in society while the American people suffer the consequences. Like mountain top coal mining that buried 2,000 miles of America's most scenic rivers and streams in the headwaters of the Appalachian Mountains.

It is time for drastic measures to decommission the 218 remaining coal burning power plants, mining processing, and transporting facilities for coal. Coal industry workers would do the decommissioning, recycling, and the environmental reclamation (estimates $100 billion) from decades of coal operations across seventeen states. The taxpayers would fund the billions needed to rid the nation of coal burning in its entirety, saving taxpayers hundreds of billions of dollars in related sickness, hospitalization, and death. Besides, coal is not competitive in the energy marketplace today at $36 per MWh without its subsidies. Solar is less expensive at $24 per MWh. You could add battery storage to provide firm power and still be cheaper given the societal costs from burning coal.

On a personal note. One day I was not feeling well and went to the doctor to get a checkup. A blood test was ordered to see if there was something amiss. The doctor's office called to say I needed to come in to review the lab results. As I sat down, the doctor asked if my wife loved me. I answered awkwardly stating yes. "Why do you ask?" I questioned. "Well, David you have elevated levels of arsenic and mercury in your blood stream." Hmm. . . I pondered. He asked if I was eating fish. Well, yes! It's the Pacific Northwest where fresh salmon is readily available. "You'd better stop eating it," he exclaimed. I should have paid closer attention at the grocery store. There were warning signs on the fish package for pregnant women not to eat the fish due to mercury.

I then remembered President Bush's environmental policy of volunteerism to reduce pollutants in the environment. Instead, coal plant smokestacks were built taller to spread the pollutants over a broader area, the idea being dilution of pollution. When George W. Bush became president, the polluting industries brought him their list of environmental regulations they wanted rolled back. They wanted an unfettered ability to maximize profits. To quote from Robert Devine's book, *Bush Versus the Environment*, "As you come to understand the means this White House employs, you'll better understand the ends that it seeks to achieve, and you'll see how the means and the ends fit together to form Bush's broad antiregulatory agenda."

Robert F. Kennedy Jr. writes in his book *Crimes Against Nature*, "George Bush and his administration have eviscerated the laws which have protected our nation's air, water, public lands, and the wildlife for the past thirty years, enriching the Presidents political contributors while lowering the quality of life for the rest of us."

President Bush obliged, abandoning public protection and market-based mechanisms, giving unfettered access to public lands and resources bought on the cheap. His administration's anti-regulatory agenda was very cleverly masked with secret behind closed door fossil fuel industry meetings headed up by Dick Cheney. They talked as though they cared about the environment, with their "Healthy Forest" initiative (code for cutting down old growth forests) and "Clear Skies" initiative (code for using the sky as a sewer).

Speaking in May, 2001, Bush said, "Our duty is to use the land well, and sometimes not to use it at all. This is our responsibility as citizens; but, more than that, it is our calling as stewards of the Earth. Good Stewardship of the environment is not just a personal responsibility, it is a public value. Americans are united in the belief that we must preserve our natural heritage and safeguard the land around us."

Beautifully put, wouldn't you say? For a President who had an antiregulatory agenda, they were words used to get elected then abandoned upon taking office. He filled the Environmental Protection Agency (E.P.A) and cabinet positions with industry insiders who methodically worked on dismantling exiting environmental protection laws, opening millions of acres of wilderness to oil, gas, and mining interests and stopped leveling fines and prosecution for industry violations of established environmental law. Bush rebuffed the Kyoto Protocol to reduce carbon emissions, abandoning all notion of conservative conservation values. Bush's corporate largess for the fossil fuel industries, mining, big Ag, big Pharma, and multiple tax cuts for his wealthy elite cost every household in American $34,000 dollars.

President Bush's Secretary of the Interior, Gale Norton who oversaw five hundred million acres of public land and 38 national parks, the National Resource Defense Council (NRDC) land program director Sharon Buccino wrote: "Gale Norton is responsible for the destruction of public wildlands and key wildlife habitat. Her goal was to give away as many of our publicly owned resources as she could to the energy, timber, and mining industries, and by that measure she was phenomenally successful. But the Interior Department's job is to protect our land, protect our drinking water sources and protect the wildlife that makes that land home. She never took that part of her job seriously. Ms. Norton said she now is setting her sights on 'the private sector.' Unfortunately, her record suggests she has been working for private special interests all along."

Ron Arnold, one of the founding members of Wise Use, said, "Our goal is to destroy, to eradicate the environmental movement. We want to be able to exploit the environment for private gain, absolutely." J. Steven Griles, former Deputy Secretary of the Department of the Interior, expanded oil and gas development on public lands, weakened environmental regulations and enforcement pertaining to mining operations and pushed for offshore drilling in California. Before leaving office, he gave a parting gift to coal companies by lowering the royalty payment to the US government. After leaving his government post he became Senior Vice President for coal giant United Company. Such industries released contamination into the environment and left the taxpayers with the related societal costs. Ergo more arsenic was released in America's rivers and streams during the Bush administration. And to think before being elected, Bush promised voters he would be their environmental President. Voters forgot to look to see where he was getting his campaign funding.

A clean, more prosperous economy requires correcting current market failures where polluters profit from environmental damage, while losses are subsidized by society at large. Most Americans understand it is unfair for industry to pass on environmental degradation and healthcare costs to taxpayers. Let us face it; Burning fossil fuel is the culprit threatening our way of life, and its societal costs are no longer bearable. It is dangerous, deadly, and finite. Air pollution kills over 8.3 million people a year world-wide. And according to the American Lung Association, over 40% of the U.S. population, 134 million people, are at risk of premature death because of chemical air pollution. The environmental and health impacts of fossil fuels disproportionately harm communities of color and low-income communities. Black, Hispanic and Latino Americans are exposed to 63% more particulate matter pollution. Minorities living in low-income areas of Louisiana known as "cancer alley" have a cancer risk 50 times higher than the national average, due to 150 nearby oil and chemical refineries. The state's legislature is allowing these companies to put profits over people's health. It is clear from the staggering societal cost burden our political system favors corporate welfare.

When fossil fuels are burned, they emit greenhouse gases like carbon dioxide that trap heat in the Earth's atmosphere and contribute to climate change. Fossil fuels account for 74% of the US greenhouse gas emissions. At least a quarter of the carbon dioxide emissions emitted from fossil fuels is absorbed by the oceans, changing their chemistry. The increased acidity makes it harder for marine organisms to build shells and coral skeletons. Ocean acidity has increased by 30% posing threats to coral reefs, fishing tourism, and the economy of coastal communities. According to the National Oceanic atmospheric administration, climate change brought upon by burning fossil fuels is contributing to more frequent extreme weather events. Extreme weather events include fires, hurricanes, flooding, and droughts.

A National Resource Defense Council report dated May 20, 2021 stated, "While critics often assert that curbing climate change would be too expensive, the cost of inaction means we're paying more than $820 billion in health costs—*every year*—from fossil fuel air pollution and climate change impacts." Another study from the Environmental and Energy Study Institute found that annual health costs of fossil burning to be $886.5 billion. Infrastructure costs and natural resource losses between 2016 and 2020 due to extreme weather events cost taxpayers an estimated at $606.9 billion. We are not going to be able to drill, frack and dig coal out of this problem of climate-altering pollution.

Society pays a heavy burden. To date 14.5 million American family homes have been damaged or destroyed from fire and floods, causing hospitalizations, serious injuries, mental health ailments, lost wages from missed days of work and early death.

Oceanic and atmospheric warming due to climate change is melting glaciers and land-based ice sheets resulting in a global sea level rise. Sea levels have risen about nine inches causing more frequent flooding, destructive storm surges and sea water intrusion.

According to Neil deGrasse Tyson, an American astrophysicist, "Sea level rise will be up to the elbow of the Statue of Liberty if all the ice caps melt."

With 40% of the US population living along the coast it is estimated that defending coastal communities from sea level rise would be astronomically impossible. In the United States 350,000 premature deaths in 2018 were attributed to fossil fuel related pollution. The highest number of deaths per capita were in Pennsylvania, Ohio, and West Virginia. If you are a resident there, you want to vote out of office recipients of fossil fuel money.

Did you know you are paying more than $20.00 for a gallon of gas! Part of that is the price per gallon at the pump and the rest is your tax dollars paying the societal burden related to health costs, ecological degradation, infrastructure destruction and subsidies to the fossil fuel industry. In other words, your tax dollars are spent on corporate socialism. According to a study by the World Bank Group titled, "Global Health Costs of PM 2.5 Air Pollution," air pollution from fine particulate matter caused 6.4 million premature deaths in 2019. Publication estimates the global cost of health damage associated with exposure to air pollution is $8.1 trillion equivalent to 6.1% of global GDP. In the United States the money spent on corporate subsidies is over $2.1 trillion annually.

That includes direct tax subsidies over $20 billion, $886.5 billion in healthcare costs, $152 to $200 billion carbon driven property damage subsidies, lost days of work productivity estimated at $50 billion, ecological devastation and infrastructure destruction, $844.5 billion. This does not include farmers, ranchers, timber landowners, and states' forest fire abatement costs per acre and loss of livestock and wildlife. This all has a drag on our economy and impacts America's GDP. Without the fossil fuel societal cost burden we could replace all gas motorized passenger vans, cars, SUVs, pickup trucks, farm machinery and construction equipment with electric motors, including installing electric charging stations in every garage. Economies of scale would drive auto costs down to be less expensive than the well-established internal combustion vehicle.

Just think! You would no longer need to buy gas, avoid engine maintenance, DEQ testing and you would have greater performance as well as peace of mind while driving, knowing you were not contributing to polluting the planet. Another fossil fuel problem is hydraulic fracking which breaks up rock formations to allow oil and gas extraction. It pollutes our air, water, land and endangers wildlife and human health. The fracking methods have been documented in 30 U.S. states and are widespread in North Dakota, Pennsylvania, and Texas. Fracking releases methane into the atmosphere and adds to the greenhouse effect. Fracking chemical wastewater was exempted from the clean water act through political maneuvering. Millions of Americans are exposed to hazardous chemicals, radioactive waste, increasing the levels of cancer and birth defects. Benzene and toluene in the dust from sand used in fracking is dangerous to health. If breathed in, it can cause leukemia and other forms of cancer. Fracking is not sustainable. A single fracking well uses thirty million gallons of water.

According to a study done by The United States House of Representative Committee on Energy and Commerce in April of 2011, between 2005 and 2009, 14 oil and gas service companies used more than 2,500 hydraulic fracking products containing 750 chemicals and other components, including the BTEX compounds-benzene, toluene, xylene, and ethylbenzene. Over all, these companies used 780 million gallons of hydraulic fracking products, not including water added at the well site. These liquid hydraulic fracking products are injected under high pressure into subterranean rocks to forcefully release natural gas. Then the wastewater is either held in contaminated surface ponds or pumped back into the ground, often contaminating ground water. As a result, nearby generational family homes, farms and ranches have had their wells rendered useless because of methane and other contaminant intrusion. Another casualty from fracking is induced earthquakes, damaging private homes, potentially affecting seven million people living in fracking zones.

The fossil fuel industry has refused to make an orderly business transition to clean fuels and renewable energy technologies. Sixty years ago, their own scientist warned about the dire effects from burning fossil fuels. They could have planted trees, added renewables to their energy portfolio and taken responsibility for operational methane leaks and capping abandoned wells. But no! Instead, they ran a deception campaign under the name "Climate Change Coalition" to undermine science and the public's understanding. Criminally and shamefully these titans of industry put profits over people's lives and wellbeing, not unlike the lies and deceit perpetrated on the American public by the tobacco industry. It is more important than ever for these companies to step up, do the right thing to become part of the solution.

All fossil fuel power generation plants and pipelines should be evaluated for methane leaks. Worldwide there are millions of orphaned oil and gas wells emitting 2.5 million tons of methane per year that need to be capped. In the US there are 3.2 million abandoned oil and gas wells emitting 281 kilotons of methane. Methane gas is a twenty-eight times more potent greenhouse gas than carbon. According to the EPA methane (CH4) accounts for about

10% of US greenhouse emissions. Globally methane is responsible for 25% of global warming. In September, 2021, the US and the EU signed the Global Methane Pledge to cut methane pollution from both energy and agricultural sources. So far one hundred nations have signed the pledge which could lower methane emissions by 30% by 2030. The extensive financial consequences of air pollution offer a direct incentive to fix the problem. Money spent reducing pollution is money saved in preventing the damage. The way to fix the problem is for politicians to advocate policies to force societal costs related to burning fossil fuels back onto the companies who sell the product.

Below is a list of the top recipients of 2024 campaign donations from the fossil fuel industry. What do they say about climate altering pollutants? Do they stand to protect the public from these deadly toxins? Or do they cater to donors' interests? I suggest you follow the money and ask your candidate, "What are you doing to protect my family from mega storms, toxins in the air, healthcare cost burdens, and environmental degradation? What is your record to date?" According to the Federal Election Commission data (released October 18, 2023) these are the campaign contribution numbers by the fossil fuel industry for the 2024 election.

Provided by Open Secrets info@opensecrets.org. The top recipients of fossil fuel dollars include: Ron DeSantis (R-FL) $349,959, August Pfluger (R-TX) $606,016, Kevin McCarthy (R-CA) $322,479, Kevin Cramer (R-ND) $412,131, Cathy McMorris Rogers (R-WA) $288,971, Steve Scalise (R-LA) $329,182, Ted Cruz (R-TX) $491,090, John Barrasso (R-WY) $335,357, Bruce Westerman (R-AR) $244,461, Niki Haley $387,729, Alfred Colin (D-TX) $243,808, Roger Wicker (R-MS) $254,204, Donald Trump (R) $845,890, Pete Ricketts (R-NE) $207,453, Jason Smith (R-MO) $164,406, Henry Cuellar (D-TX) $162,413, Garnet Graves (R-LA) $152,550, Tony Gonzales (R-TX) $263,528, Ryan Zinke (R-MT) $216,055, Mike Johnson (R-LA) $325,795.

We need legislative reform to phase out subsidies to the fossil fuel industry, not pay lawmakers to keep business as usual going, leading the world down the path of extinction. Doing so would save taxpayers billions of dollars and correct market intervention inefficiencies. This should be a priority for federal policymakers to accelerate Americas transition to the clean energy economy. The electrification of our transportation system with less expensive clean power generation is already demonstrating the replacement feasibility of fossil fuels, as witnessed by growing market share from the sale of electric cars, trucks, buses, solar and wind power plants, biofuels, geothermal, hydrogen fuels, energy storage and power plants with zero emissions. We need to place public health before profits and work together to replace oil and gas with renewable energy technologies, hydrogen fuel cells and photosynthesis-based biofuels. As well as new technology innovations currently in various stages of commercialization.

CHAPTER 5

Koch Industries, Inc.

"There is no other corporation in the United States in my view that is unabashedly bare knuckle aggressive across the board about its own self-interest. Its non-profits gave 30.5 million to 221 universities for curriculums that support their real-world view. They have been buying off universities and infiltrating the curriculum of elementary schools. They take credit for the culture of climate denial that now permeates the Republican Party."

—Charles Lewis, Founder of the Center for Public Integrity

I have singled out Koch Industries Inc. for their political meddling and aggressive influence on American politics. This by no means lets the "Big Oil Titans," Exxon Mobile, Chevron, Shell, BP, Eni, and Total Energies off the hook for their climate altering pollution and disinformation campaigns. Koch Industries has funded non-profits like Americans for Prosperity to influence election outcomes. They also provide funding for the Cato Institute, the Federalist Society, and the Heritage foundation. Koch Industries has single handedly taken over the Republican party to protect the company's fossil fuel interests, preventing any legislation to mitigate climate altering pollution and instead forcing the US treasury to pay for their toxic emissions. Republicans are enabling the highest level of corporate welfare over public health and safety.

According to a recent article in Sustainable Business, since 2008, 411 politicians have signed the Koch no climate action pledge. Koch's influence is extremely far reaching. The entire House Republican leadership, twenty-six senators and 140 house members are signatories. Signatories include former Governor Scott Walker in Wisconsin, gubernatorial candidate Ken Cuccinelli in Virginia, Florida's attorney general Pam Bondi—eight governors and hundreds of state legislators.

This is what the pledge says:

> I ________________________, pledge to the taxpayers of the state of ______________
>
> And to the American people I will oppose any legislation relating to climate change that includes a net increase in government revenues.

Any legislation on climate change that enacts fees would have to be offset by other tax cuts. Why this language? Because any sane climate policy would involve increasing costs on polluters and directing revenues to clean technologies. The pledge ties the hands of legislators as it is intended. According to the "Investigating Reporter Workshop" which tracks the pledge, seventy-six out of eighty-five republican freshmen signed it as candidates in 2010 and 57 of them received campaign contributions from Koch Industries' political action committee. These freshmen Republicans have helped cut the budget for the Environmental Protection Agency, challenged any attempt to issue new regulations and prevented policies which would address climate change by federal agencies. The Workshop Report indicated their top priority includes promoting American consumption of oil and gas, while blaming environmental laws for hurting the economy and questioning the science behind global warming.

- According to a Greenpeace 44-page article titled "Koch Industries Secretly Funded the Climate Denial Machine," from 2005 to 2008 Koch Industries Inc. funded climate opposition groups to the tune of $24,888,283 and funded direct lobbying efforts of $37,960,000. According to the Federal Energy Agency Koch Industries committed fraud, made false claims, and engaged in bribery, price fixing and other corrupt practices. Here are just some examples of Koch Industries record on Environmental Crimes and Violations:

- In 2009 the US Justice Department and the EPA announced that Koch Industries' Invista subsidiary would pay a $1.7 million penalty and spend $500 million to fix environmental violations at facilities in seven states in an agreement with the US EPA and Department of Justice.
- Leaks on Koch-operated oil pipelines have resulted in major spills in Minnesota in recent years. In December, 2009 Koch's pipeline spilled 210,000 gallons of crude oil in Philbrook Minnesota, another in 2005 spilled over 100,000 gallons in Little Falls MN.
- In May of 2001 Koch Industries paid twenty-five million to settle with the US government for illegally accounting for oil removed from federal lands.
- In late 2000 the company was charged with covering up the illegal release of 91 tons of known carcinogen benzene from its refinery in Corpus Christi, thereby facing a 97-count formal accusation with potential fines of $350 million. Koch cut a deal with Bush Attorney General John Ashcroft to drop all major charges. In exchange for a guilty plea for falsifying documents Koch paid a $20 million settlement.
- In 2000 EPA fined Koch industries thirty million dollars for its role in three hundred oil spills that resulted in more

than 3 million gallons of crude oil leaking into ponds, lakes, and coastal waters.

- In 1999 Koch Industries' subsidiary pleaded guilty to charges it had negligently allowed aviation fuel to leak into waters near the Mississippi River from its refinery in Rosemont Minnesota and it had illegally dumped a million gallons of high ammonia wastewater onto the ground and into the Mississippi River.

- Koch negligence towards environmental safety led to tragic loss of life in 1996. A rusty and corroded Koch pipeline leaked flammable butane near a Texas residential neighborhood. Warned by the smell of the gas, two teenagers drove their truck toward the nearest payphone to call for help but they never made it. Sparks from their truck ignited the gas cloud and the two were burned alive. The National Transportation Safety board determined the probable cause of the accident was the failure of Koch to adequately protect its pipeline from corrosion and the ineffectiveness of the Koch program to educate residents about how to respond during a pipeline leak.

In total since 2,000, Koch Industries has been fined $1,014,704,033 racking up 475 different violations, including environmental, employment, workplace safety, health and consumer protection violations, price fixing or anti-competitive practices and energy market violations. The violations and related fines were just a cost of doing business to make billions more at the expense of others. Koch Industries is a real and present danger to America, and in sixty countries around the world where they do business. Congressional leadership should be protecting Americans from debilitating health outcomes, environmental degradation, and loss of life. Most polluters do not pay for their heavy burden on society with their destructive climate alerting pollution. Koch Industries is a good example of why we need a strong regulatory government to protect us. Polluting industries' behavior mandates appropriate regulations to stop their malfeasance. Koch Industries is a bad actor ignoring corporate responsibility, public health, and safety. Charles Koch in a speech declared that equal opportunity laws, wage rules, and health and safety laws were inherently anti-capitalist, and that the business community was not committed to free enterprise because it went along with pesky regulations like workplace hazard, and minimum wage rules.

For decades, the Koch Brothers had been funding front groups including Citizens for a Sound Economy (CSE), a wholly owned subsidiary of Koch Industries. Over time a Koch Industries funded national agenda emerged to take over the republican party. Designed to advance Koch Industries' self-interests and free market beliefs, it resulted in the anti-tax, ant regulation, and anti-government Tea Party movement. This libertarian free market "Tea Party" revolt communicated their demands with such slogans as "Don't Tread on Me," "Enough is Enough," "Kick Government Off Our Backs," and "Citizens Against Regressive Taxation." The letters T-E-A were used by some protesters to form the acronym "Taxed Enough Already."

On the historical deadline of April 15th for filing individual income tax returns, a nationwide rally across 750 cities drew 250,000 people. Tax Day became a populace social and political movement advocating for a national economy operating without government oversight. The movement's goals included limiting the size of the federal government, reducing government spending, lowering the national debt, and opposing tax increases. The Koch Industries Tea Party participants hailed themselves as heirs to the American Revolution, akin to the Tea Act of 1773. The November 2010 midterms promised to be the referendum as much on the Tea Party as on Barack Obama, particularly since there was a continued push pull relationship between the Tea Party and the Republican Party. The party candidates won endorsements from Republican groups, while others provoked backlash from the Republican establishment.

Longtime Republicans, a number of whom had lost to Tea Party candidates in their primary races, chose to contest the general election as independents. In the end, it seemed that the Tea Party label mattered less than the strength of an individual candidate.

In Jeff Nesbit's book, "Poison Tea-How Big Oil and Big Tobacco Invented the Tea Party and Captured the GOP," he describes how the long rise of the Tea Party movement was orchestrated. The goal was to raise a billion dollars to successfully bend one of the two national parties to their liking with libertarian free market principles at its center. Its aim was to break Washington, as America saw in the debt ceiling debacle of 2011, prompted by the Republican party's demand that President Barrack Obama negotiate over deficit reduction and a maximum amount of money that U.S. Treasury was allowed to borrow. There are no mistakes or accidents in the Tea Party movement. Its leadership made certain of that with the help of the Citizens for a Sound Economy (CSE) they reached beyond Koch oil money for their new grassroots efforts. They partnered with Phillip Morris and RJ Reynolds money to create anti-tax front groups in a handful of states that would battle any tax that emerged. It would make no difference what kind of tax the front groups could battle. Cigarette excise taxes, refined oil fees, any tax for any purpose was bad.

At its core this was the beginning of the American Tea Party revolt against the power of the government. They recruited average citizens from a variety of ideological groups to their causes. They worked side by side with corporations, directed workers and employees to provide boots on the ground. The public would not know until years later that the Tea Party anti-tax, anti-regulation, anti-government revolt was financed by Philip Morris and RJ Reynolds, and Koch Industries under the guise of political and business coalitions. The Tea Party movement looked an awful lot like the efforts to kill the Clinton/Gore British thermal unit (BTU) tax rate. The tax was to be levied on coal, natural gas, liquid petroleum gases, gasoline, nuclear generated electricity, hydroelectricity, and imported electricity at a base rate of 25.7 cents per million BTU, with an additional 34.2 cents per million BTU on unrefined petroleum products. The tax would have taxed all fuel sources based on their heat content. The U.S. consumes over 100 quadrillion BTUs of energy annually. This tax would have gone a long way to fix market-based economics and make the polluters pay for their costly climate-altering pollution. Koch Industries with their front group Americans for Prosperity (AFP) can be attributed to killing this tax on polluters.

I want to remind voters that tax revenues go into the government coffers. This money can be spent on the general welfare of the nation, or it can go to corporate interests like Koch Industries in the form of societal cost subsidies to already wealthy individuals. Or it can go toward public good, such as health care, public education, a living wage, job retraining, ecological restoration, public safety, improved towns, city infrastructure and technology transition to the newly emerging clean economy and much more, whatever benefits the general welfare of the nation.

So, vote out of office all republicans and democrats who have sided with the polluters. Your life may depend on it! You deserve to have a government of, for and by the people. Support legislation requiring polluters to pay to clean up our air, land, and waterways. Require stricter government-imposed safety standards on pipelines and production facilities and hefty fines for violations. Impose a $75 per ton charge on carbon emissions with the revenue offsetting individual payroll taxes, direct payment to taxpayers or investment tax credits to buy an electric vehicle. The fossil fuel industry has for decades lied, deceived the American people, and refused to make an orderly transition to clean energy alternatives. The time has come to make the polluters pay so you do not have to!

CHAPTER 6

Climate Alerting Pollution Sold as a Hoax

"The era of procrastination of half-measures soothing and baffling expedients of delays is coming to its close. In its place were entering a period of consequences".

—Winston Churchill

It's mid-February, already the vegetation is in bloom. Crocuses are flowering two months before the start of Spring. Last summer, record temperatures reached 114 degrees turning the tips of evergreen trees a burnt orange. My blueberries looked like hanging dried raisins. Baby bird nestlings struggled out of their nests to escape the record heat, falling to the ground to die or eaten by predators. Most likely a few baby chicks survived. More drought conditions resulted in more summer fires. Sea level is rising on the Oregon coast.

Let us fully examine what is behind the phrase, "Climate change is a hoax." Why are politicians making this statement? What is the benefit in getting you to believe that climate change is a hoax? Who profits from having us divided and polarized? Why do they say, *I do not know, I am not a scientist*? Why did Trump abandon the Paris Climate Accord? Was it really going to hurt the American economy and be a job killer? Does it give other nations an economic advantage? Of course not. None of these job killing, economic disadvantage or financial ruin statements are true. Is there deception and concealment going on? Absolutely! What could these politicians be hiding and do not want you to know or pay attention to?

The following is a perfect example of how fossil fuel companies have a hold on our policy makers and the communication framing which goes along with it. House Republicans on March 30, 2023 approved a sprawling energy package that seeks to undo all President Joe Biden's agenda to address climate change. The legislation would sharply increase domestic production of oil, natural gas, and coal and ease permitting restrictions that delay pipelines, refineries, and other products. Biden threatened to veto the bill, saying it would replace "pro consumer policies" adopted in the bipartisan landmark climate law approved last year. The Republican's bill was named "The Lower Energy Cost Act." They gave it the symbolic label HR 1- the top legislative priority of the new GOP majority which took control of the House in January 2022. Democrats viewed their bill as a thinly veiled license to pollute. The bill would roll back investments in clean energy and "pad oil and gas company profits," the White House said.

The measure combined dozens of separate proposals and represented more than two years of work by the Republicans who chafed at Biden's environmental agenda. They said Biden's efforts thwarted US energy production and increased costs at gas pumps and grocery stores. "Families are struggling because of President Biden's war on American energy," said House Majority Leader Steve Scalise, R-LA, one of the bills main sponsors. The GOP bill "will unleash abundant U.S. natural resources so we can produce energy in America," Scalise said. "We do not have to be addicted to foreign countries that do not like us.

Democrats called the bill a giveaway to big oil companies. "Republicans refuse to hold polluters accountable for the damage they caused to our air, our water, our communities and our climate," said New Jersey representative Frank Pallone, the top Democrat on the House Energy and Commerce committee. "While Democrats delivered historic wins for American people by passing historic climate legislation, Republicans are actively working to undermine that progress and do the bidding of their polluter friends," said Pallone.

Democrats called Republican statements misleading and said the GOP plan was a thinly disguised effort to reward oil companies and other energy producers that have contributed millions of dollars to GOP campaigns. Arizona Representative Raul Grijalva, the top Democrat on the House Natural Resources Committee, derided the bill as the "Polluters Over People Act" and "a nearly 200-page love letter to the polluting industries." Instead of reining in "Big Oil" companies that have reported record profits while "hoarding thousands of unused leases" on public lands and waters, the GOP bill lowers royalty rates paid by energy producers and reinstates noncompetitive leasing of public lands," Grijalva said.

The bill also gives mining companies "carte blanche" access to our public lands and "makes a mockery of tribal consultation" required under federal law, he said. Under the GOP plan, mining companies will "destroy sacred and special places" throughout the west, "ruin the landscape and leave behind a toxic mess that pollutes our water and hurts our health—all without paying a cent to the American people," Grijalva said.

Senate Majority Leader Schumer called the measure "a giveaway to big oil pretending to be an energy package." He said the house energy package "would gut important environmental safeguards on fossil fuel projects," locking America "into expensive, erratic and dirty energy sources while setting us back more than a decade on our transition to clean energy."

Schumer said he supports streamlining the nation's cumbersome permitting process for energy projects, especially those that would deliver "clean energy" such as wind solar and geothermal power. "But the republican plan falls woefully short on this front as well," he said, calling on the Republicans to back reforms that would help ease the transition to renewable energy and accelerate construction of transmission lines to bolster the nation's aging power grid. Schumer and other Democrats said the Republican bill would repeal a new $27 billion dollar Greenhouse Gas Reduction Fund and other parts of the clean climate and health care law passed by Democrats last year. The bill would also eliminate a new tax on methane pollution.

Four Democrats voted in favor of the HR-1 bill. They are Reps. Henry Cuellar and Vincente Gonzalez of Texas, Jared Golden of Maine, and Marie Gluesenkamp Perez of Washington state. They should go on your list to be voted out of office. Rep. Brian Fitzpatrick, R-Pa., was the only Republican to oppose the bill. Way to go Brian.

An article published on October 28, 2021, by Benjamin Franta from Stanford University illustrated a pattern of secrecy and cover up by the fossil fuel industry. As far back as 1959 he found a transcript of an "Energy and Man Symposium" held at Columbia University in New York. Edward Teller in his speech warned oil industry executives stating," Whenever you burn conventional fuel you create carbon dioxide. Its presence in the atmosphere causes the greenhouse effect. If the world kept using fossil fuels, the ice caps would begin to melt, raising sea level. Eventually, all the coastal cities would be covered," he warned.

Benjamin Franta noted this speech was given before the moon landing, before the Beatles first single, before Martin Luther King's "I Have a Dream" speech, before the first modern aluminum can was ever made. In 1965 the President of the American Petroleum Institute, Frank Ikard referenced a report called "Restoring the Quality of Our Environment" and told the industry audience, "There is still time to save the world's peoples from the catastrophic consequences of pollution, but time is running out." He continued that, "One of the most important predictions of the report is that carbon dioxide is being added to the earth's atmosphere by the burning of coal, oil, and natural gas at such a rate that by the year 2000 the heat balance will be so modified as to possibly cause marked changes in climate." Frank Ikard noted the report had found that "nonpolluting means of powering automobiles, buses and trucks is likely to become a national necessity."

On October 16, 1979, a memo about a study done by Steve Knisely warned about fossil fuel combustion releasing CO2 concentrations into the atmosphere stating that carbon levels would reach 400 PPM by 2010. "The potential problem is great and urgent."

In 1980 John Laurmann from Stanford University presented a slide to the American Petroleum Institute's climate change task force warning of globally catastrophic effects from continued fossil fuel use.

In 1981 Roger Cohen from Exxon reported in an internal memo that the company's long-term business plans could "produce effects which will indeed be catastrophic (at least for a substantial fraction of the earth's population)."

In 1982, M.B. Glaser, Exxon's, Manager of the Environmental Affairs Programs submitted a 46-page report which included a technical review called "CO2 Greenhouse Effects" warning about the effects of continued burning of fossil fuels altering our climate and its effect on society.

In 1986, the Dutch oil company Shell, finished an internal confidential report that was uncovered in 2018 by Jelmer Mommers, a Dutch journalist. It predicted global warming from fossil fuels would cause changes which would be "the greatest in recorded history," including "destructive floods and abandonment of entire countries and even forced migration around the world."

What did the oil industry do with these revelations? In short, there was a coordinated effort to sow doubt about climate change to block clean energy legislation and climate treaties. These efforts to sow doubt gained enormous influence through the industry-funded entity called "Global Climate Coalition." Its members consisted of a round table of polluters. Fast forward to October 28, 2021, at the Congressional subcommittee questioning oil executives from Exxon, BP, Shell, and the American Petroleum Institute about the industry's efforts to downplay the role of fossil fuels in climate change. Exxon CEO Darren Woods told lawmakers that his company's public statements "are and have always been truthful" and the company does not spread disinformation regarding climate change.

Okay, I get it. Exxon public statements have been truthful-maybe. The operative word is "public" and maybe the company does not spread disinformation. But that's where front groups like the Global Climate Coalition come into play. These organizations can tell lies and spread misinformation. Exxon Mobile contributed money to organizations including $36 million paid into the US Chamber of Commerce (non-governmental). All promoted climate denial propaganda.

Koch Industry lobbyists worked hard to stop the Biden administration's Build Back Better legislation, precisely because it was designed to curtail future growth of the fossil fuel industry to prevent more societal costs on the American people.

The king pin funding climate denial is the Koch Family Foundation at $123 million. As mentioned earlier, through their Americans for Prosperity Foundation, 411 office holders including 26 US Senators and 144 house members all signed that no carbon tax pledge in violation of their oath of office and sworn duty to the US Constitution. Koch Industries' egregious actions have had a serious negative impact on the American family, essentially killing any climate change legislation. Other contributors are Scaife Foundations $39.6 million, Bradley Foundation $29.6 million, Howard Charitable Foundation $24.8 million, John William Pope Foundations $21.9, Searle Freedom Trust $21.7 million, the John Templeton Foundation $20.2 million, and Exxon Mobil $36 million.

Other contributors include:

Mercatus Center, Georgetown University, Americans for Prosperity Foundation (AFP), Heritage Foundation, Citizens for a Sound Economy Foundation, Federalist Society for Law and Public Policy Studies, Texas Public Policy Foundation, Stata Policy, Inc., Manhattan Institute for Policy Research, and the American

Legislative Exchange Council. All provided funding to downplay the effects of burning fossil fuels.

To summarize, coal interests, mining, auto, oil, and gas companies have spent millions to confuse the public and block any efforts to curtail the pollution-affecting climate change to protect their bottom lines. They secretly promoted climate denial to block any legislation to reign in their business-as-usual practices.

Politicians who have stated climate change is a hoax, including former President Trump, have received money from the fossil fuel industry. They do not want you to connect the dots. They have deceived you. They are not serving your best interests. The fossil fuel industry knew and has always known—yet deceived the public for over 60 years—that burning fossil fuel destroys the planet! Currently twenty-four lawsuits are underway to hold these companies responsible for their crimes against humanity. The industry has recklessly left thousands of abandoned wells leaking methane gas, a greenhouse accelerator. The fossil fuel industry has had years to transition to clean energy sources but failed to do so.

In the meantime, the American taxpayer subsidizes the industry. Your elected officials should have been passing legislation to force the industry to transition in a timely manner to the emerging clean economy. Today there are eleven million jobs in the dirty inflationary fossil fuels industry, compared to thirty-eight million clean energy jobs being created by 2030 and 46 million jobs by 2050. The clean energy economy can put the dirty fuel industries in the rearview mirror. We need a more rapid transmission to clean energy so we can end the burdensome societal costs.

My fellow Americans, you have been lied to by the very people you are supposed to trust, tricked into believing something that is not true, deceived through concealment and made unknowing participants in preventing action on climate change. You have been paying the price through loss of life, property damage and the fleecing of our treasury to support an industry that has failed America and your family. It is unfortunate when you realize the environmental destruction to the Goldilocks planet that has taken place over the past decades that could have been avoided—the human death toll, homes flooded and burned down, species loss by the billions and the financial burden born by all.

In contrast, the clean energy economy provides clean air, water, and food as well as energy independence from fossil fuels' climate altering pollution. This includes geothermal, solar, wind, biomass, battery storage for intermittent energy supply and clean fuels such as hydrogen-based fuel cells. There is a choice to be made. You can have a drill baby drill policy coupled with deregulation policies, letting industry pollute our environment and destroy the planet in the process, or be an informed voter, voting for only those politicians who advocate for clean energy technology solutions.

If a politician says climate change is a hoax or "I am not a scientist," he is either ill-informed or is being funded by the fossil fuel industry. In either case he should not get your vote and if he or she is in office they should be voted out of office. Fix this problem by electing individuals who openly advocate for the transition to a clean economy. Today electric cars, trucks, motorcycles, recreational vehicles, jet skis, boats, bicycles, skateboards, landscaping equipment and electric walking shoes are all affordable and available in the market.

This moment in time calls for an all-hands-on deck response for you to do something. You could buy less gasoline, i.e., trip consolidation, less car idling, good tire pressure, carpooling, mass transit, bike or walk more. At home take steps to reduce your energy consumption. You can participate in local energy efficiency programs designed to make your home consume less energy. Your home will be more comfortable and have a higher resale value as a result. All these efforts will save you money and reduce carbon emissions at the same time. You could buy an electric vehicle. If not new, buy used. Get rid of your internal combustion engine, as it will soon become a stranded asset.

Enjoy the quiet, clean, regular maintenance-free electric vehicle. Pay less than $2 per gallon equivalent for electric charging with zero emissions. And most important of all, vote corrupt and deceptive politicians who knowingly told you climate change was a hoax out of office, regardless of the “R” or “D” beside their names. Only vote for candidates who will pass legislation to abate climate altering pollution. In the next chapter, I have provided a list of House Representatives and Senators who are climate deniers plus signatories to the Koch Industry no-climate-tax pledge which has been tied to congressional climate inaction. Also, the list of senators who signed a letter to President Trump to abandon the Paris Climate Agreement.

CHAPTER 7

Time to Drain the Swamp

"Let us just say it. The Republicans are the problem. The GOP has become an insurgent outlier in American politics. It is ideologically extreme; scornful of compromise; unmoved by conventional understanding of the facts, evidence, and science and dismissive of the legitimacy of its political opposition. The extreme elements within the Republican Party need to be removed."

—Thomas Mann and Norm Ornstein op-ed Washington Post

In World War II Japanese soldiers occupied the island of Ramree. The Japanese soldiers survived there by eating the local wildlife, denying the local saltwater crocodiles their food source. The crocodiles with no food were forced into hibernation called "estivation." The British 14th Army of the Burma campaign offensive were ordered to take the island. One thousand Japanese soldiers were forced into the Mangrove swamps, only to be met by an army of ferociously hungry saltwater crocodiles. According to the Guinness World Records it was the greatest disaster suffered by humans from animals. Of the one thousand soldiers retreating into the Mangrove swamps only twenty survived.

It's time to drain the swamp in Washington on a mass scale. Vote to expel those who betrayed your trust and undermined your rights and your family's wellbeing. You have a civic duty, a responsibility to do the right thing. You do not need swamp crocodiles to fix this. Just be an educated voter. Do not vote for individuals peddling divisive slogans but meaningful policies. Vote to put out of office those who lack moral courage, integrity and are absent of admirable principles. Vote in individuals who have a stated policy agenda to address climate altering pollution.

Once we vote the bad actors out of office, we need to select the right candidates to end a repeating cycle of dishonest power-hungry individuals. Brain Klaas author of "Why Did We Get the Wrong Leaders" and "Corruptible: Who Gets Power and How it Changes Us," asks four questions. Do worse people get power? Does power make people worse? Why do we let people control us who clearly have no business being in control? How can we ensure that incorruptible people get power instead? There is a certain kind of person who is particularly good at getting power and there is also a certain kind of person that is good at staying in power. Brian Klaas studied bad people who do terrible things in power and about power corrupting, which it does. He explored hidden factors that are often ignored to our own peril and detriment because the systems around positions of power affect outcomes. They are important because they are the things you can fix most easily. It is hard to change the magnetism of power. It is hard to change the way that power changes people's psychology and their neurology. What is easier to change is the systems we design that determine who ends up in power.

Brian Klaas explains the political system works by self-selection bias. Selection bias is tied to power. It is the idea that we wait for people to say, *I should be powerful.* We wait for people to say *I am the one who should be in charge.* That is self-selection bias selecting people who are power hungry. We have a democratic responsive government which is supposed to do what we say, and they are supposed to be elected by us and yet consistently we pick snakes in suits whom we know are not good. We make irrational decisions when it comes to whom we choose to be in power for no reason other than their height and facial features, which is incredibly stupid. Psychopaths are a real problem when it comes to positions of power. A psychopath is someone who might not look like a psychopath. Psychopaths are good at blending in and looking like everybody else. They are superficially charming and likeable, so they do not have to show effective leadership qualities or traits that are tied to good public servant leadership.

Given the history of American politics and how easy it is for unethical people to be elected to public office, it is time to set qualifying parameters for anyone seeking an office, thereby avoiding George Santos type characters. Let us start vetting a person's background by a third party attesting to its authenticity. Require a government civic test and psychological behavioral test, thereby avoiding electing dishonest, psychopathic crazies and people lacking moral character.

The following is a list of Senators and House Representatives who have violated their oaths of office, first, by refusing to approve the 2020 election certification of the Joe Biden win. Despite having full knowledge and absolute evidence that no voter fraud took place to alter the election, all of which was substantiated by 61courts, US Attorney General Bill Barr (Trump appointee), as well as the election outcomes certified by 50 Secretaries of State. Secondly, for signing the Koch Industries pledge for no tax on climate change legislation. Third, for engaging in political rhetoric, fabricating lies with willful intent to deceive the public. These actions reflect a lack of integrity, are unethical, immoral and are juxtaposed to their sworn oaths of office. They sold out to the corporate welfare elite to maintain their personal power, political status, congressional pay, and privileges, while failing to enact policies to better the lives of everyday Americans.

> These elected officials are precisely what Thomas Paine warned us about in his 1737 "Common Sense" publication. *"Interested men who are not to be trusted, weak men who cannot see; prejudiced men who will not see; and a certain set of moderate men. . .will be the cause of more calamities to this continent than all the other three."*

Senators who refused to certify the 2020 election.

Ted Cruz (TX)
Josh Hawley (MO)
Cindy Hyde-Smith (MS)
Cynthia Lummis (WY)
John Kennedy (LA)
Roger Marshall (KS)
Rick Scott (FL)
Tommy Tuberville (AL)

House members who refused to certify the 2020 election.

Robert Aderholt (AL)
Rick Allen (GA)
Jodey Arrington (TX)
Brian Babin (TX)
Jim Baird (IN)
Jim Banks (IN)
Cliff Bentz (OR)
Jack Bergman (MI)
Stephanie Bice (OK)
Andy Biggs (AZ)
Dan Bishop (NC)
Lauren Boebert (CO)
Mike Bost (IL)
Mo Brooks (AL)
Ted Budd (NC)
Tim Burchett (TN)
Michael Burgess (TX)
Ken Calvert (CA)
Kat Cammack (FL)
Jerry Carl (AL)
Buddy Carter (GA)
John Carter (TX)
Madison Cawthorn (NC)
Steve Chabot (OH)
Ben Cline (VA)
Michael Cloud (TX)
Andrew Clyde (GA)
Tom Cole (OK)
Rick Crawford (AR)
Warren Davidson (OH)
Scott DesJarlais (TN)
Mario Diaz-Balart (FL)
Byron Donalds (FL)
Jeff Duncan (SC)

Neal Dunn (FL)
Ron Estes (KS)
Pat Fallon (TX)
Michelle Fischbach (MN)
Scott Fitzgerald (WI)
Chuck Fleischmann (TN)
Virginia Foxx (NC)
Scott Franklin (FL)
Russ Fulcher (ID)
Matt Gaetz (FL)
Mike Garcia (CA)
Bob Gibbs (OH)
Carlos Gimenez (FL)
Louie Gohmert (TX)
Bob Good (VA)
Lance Gooden (TX)
Paul Gosar (AZ)
Garret Graves (LA)
Sam Graves (MO)
Mark Green (TN)
Marjorie Greene (GA)
Morgan Griffith (VA)
Michael Guest (MS)
Jim Hagedorn (MN)
Andy Harris (MD)
Diana Harshbarger (TN)
Vicky Hartzler (MO)
Kevin Hern (OK)
Yvette Herrell (NM)
Jody Hice (GA)
Clay Higgins (LA)
Richard Hudson (NC)
Darrell Issa (CA)
Ronny Jackson (TX)
Chris Jacobs (NY)
Mike Johnson (LA)
Bill Johnson (OH)
Jim Jordan (OH)
John Joyce (PA)
Fred Keller (PA)
Trent Kelly (MS)
Mike Kelly (PA)
David Kustoff (TN)
Doug LaMalfa (CA)
Doug Lamborn (CO)
Jacob LaTurner (KS)
Debbie Lesko (AZ)
Billy Long (MO)
Barry Loudermilk (GA)
Frank Lucas (OK)
Blaine Luetkemeyer (MO)
Nicole Malliotakis (NY)
Tracey Mann (KS)
Brian Mast (FL)
Kevin McCarthy (CA)
Lisa McClain (MI)
Daniel Meuser (PA)
Mary Miller (IL)
Carol Miller (WV)
Alex Mooney (WV)
Barry Moore (AL)
Markwayne Mullin (OK)
Gregory Murphy (NC)
Troy Nehls (TX)

Ralph Norman (SC)
Devin Nunes (CA)
Jay Obernolte (CA)
Burgess Owens (UT)
Steven Palazzo (MS)
Gary Palmer (AL)
Greg Pence (IN)
Scott Perry (PA)
August Pfluger (TX)
Bill Posey (FL)
Guy Reschenthaler (PA)
Tom Rice (SC)
Mike Rogers (AL)
Hal Rogers (KY)
John Rose (TN)
Matt Rosendale (MT)
David Rouzer (NC)
John Rutherford (FL)
Steve Scalise (LA)
David Schweikert (AZ)
Pete Sessions (TX)
Jason Smith (MO)
Adrian Smith (NE)
Lloyd Smucker (PA)
Elise Stefanik (NY)
Greg Steube (FL)
Chris Stewart (UT)
Glenn Thompson (PA)
Tom Tiffany (WI)
William Timmons (SC)
Jefferson Van Drew (NJ)
Beth Van Duyne (TX)
Tim Walberg (MI)
Jackie Walorski (IN)
Randy Weber (TX)
Daniel Webster (FL)
Roger Williams (TX)
Joe Wilson (SC)
Rob Wittman (VA)
Ron Wright (TX)
Lee Zeldin (NY)

THE HOUSE OF REPRESENTATIVES CLIMATE SCIENCE DENIERS and House members who signed the Koch Industries "No Climate Tax Pledge" thus preventing any legislation to stop pollution altering climate change.

Alabama—Robert Aderholt
Alabama—Dale Strong
Alabama—Gary Palmer

Arizona—Paul Gosar
Arizona—Andy Biggs
Arizona—David Schweikert
Arizona—Debbie Lesko

Arkansas—Rick Crawford
Arkansas—Steve Womack

Arkansas—Bruce Westerman

California—Doug LaMalfa
California—Tom McClintock
California—David Valadao
California—Kevin McCarthy
California—Ken Calvert
California—Darrell Issa

Colorado—Lauren Boebert
Colorado—Ken Buck
Colorado—Doug Lamborn

Florida—Neal Dunn
Florida—Kat Cammack
Florida—Aaron Bean
Florida—John Rutherford
Florida—Cory Mills
Florida—Bill Posey
Florida—Daniel Webster
Florida—Laurel Lee
Florida—Mario Diaz-Balart

Georgia—Barry Loudermilk
Georgia—Rich McCormick
Georgia—Austin Scott
Georgia—Andrew Clyde
Georgia—Mike Collins
Georgia—Rick Allen
Georgia—Marjorie Taylor Green

Idaho—Michael K. Simpson
Idaho—Russ Fulcher

Illinois—Mike Bost
Illinois—Mary Miller
Illinois—Darin LaHood

Indiana—Rudy Yakym
Indiana—Jim Banks
Indiana—Larry Bucshon

Kentucky—James Comer Jr.
Kentucky—Thomas Massie

Louisiana—Steve Scalise
Louisiana—Clay Higgins
Louisiana—Mike Johnson
Louisiana—Julia Letlow

Maryland—Andrew Harris

Michigan—Bill Huizenga
Michigan—Tim Walberg
Michigan—Fred Upton
Michigan—John James

Minnesota—Tom Emmer
Minnesota—Pete Stauber

Missouri—Ann Wagner
Missouri—Blaine Luetkemeyer
Missouri—Mark Alford
Missouri—Jason Smith

Nebraska—Mike Flood
Nebraska—Don Bacon
Nebraska—Adrian Smith

Nevada—Mark Amodei

New York—Nick LaLota
New York—George Santos
New York—Nick Langworthy

North Carolina—Virginia Foxx
North Carolina—David Rouzer
North Carolina—Richard Hudson
North Carolina—Patrick McHenry
North Carolina—Chuck Edwards

North Dakota—Kelly Armstrong

Ohio—Bill Johnson
Ohio—Max Miller
Ohio—Warren Davidson
Ohio—Mike Carey

Oklahoma—Kevin Hern
Oklahoma—Josh Brecheen
Oklahoma—Frank Lucas

Pennsylvania—Scott Perry
Pennsylvania—John Joyce
Pennsylvania—Glenn Thompson

South Carolina—Joe Wilson
South Carolina—Jeff Duncan

Tennessee—Tim Burchett
Tennessee—Chuck Fleischmann
Tennessee—Andy Ogles

Texas—Dan Crenshaw
Texas—Keith Self
Texas—Lance Gooden
Texas—Morgan Luttrell
Texas—Michael McCaul
Texas—August Pluger
Texas—Randy Weber
Texas—Jodey Arrington
Texas—Chip Roy
Texas—Troy Nehls
Texas—Michael C. Burgess
Texas—John Carter
Texas—Brian Babin

Utah—Chris Stewart

Virginia—Rob Wittman
Virginia—H. Morgan Griffith

Washington—Cathy McMorris Rodgers

West Virginia—Carol Miller

West Virginia—Alex Mooney

Wisconsin—Glenn Grothman

Wisconsin—Tom Tiffany

Wyoming—Harriet Hageman

THE SENATE CLIMATE SCIENCE DENIERS who signed the Koch Industries "No Climate Tax Pledge" thus preventing any legislation to stop pollution altering climate change.

Alabama—Tommy Tuberville
Alaska—Dan Sullivan
Arkansas—Tom Cotton
Florida—Marco Rubio
Indiana—Todd Young, Mike Braun
Iowa—Joni Ernst, Chuck Grassley
Kansas—Roger Marshall, Jerry Moran
Kentucky—Mitch McConnell, Rand Paul
Louisiana—Bill Cassidy, John N. Kennedy
Mississippi—Roger Wicker, Cindy Hyde-Smith
Missouri—Eric Schmitt, Josh Hawley
Montana—Steve Daines
Nebraska—Deb Fischer
North Carolina—Thom Tillis, Tedd Budd
North Dakota—John Hoeven, Kevin Cramer
Ohio—J.D. Vance
Oklahoma—James Lankford, Markwayne Mullin
South Dakota—John Thune
Tennessee—Marsha Blackburn, Bill Hagerty
Texas—Ted Cruz. John Cornyn
Utah—Mike Lee

West Virginia—Shelly Moore Capito
Wisconsin—Ron Johnson
Wyoming—John Barrasso, Cynthia Lummis

The following is a list of senators who signed a letter to President Trump requesting he abandon the international partnership to address climate altering pollution reduction, the "Paris Climate Accord." After each name is the amount of money each senator received from the fossil fuel industry which has the appearance of a "Quid Pro Quo" exchange. According to an article in "The Guardian" twenty-two republican signatories received a total sum of $10,694,284 from the fossil fuel industry. Broken down as follows:

John Barrasso (R-WY)-$585,950
Jim Inhofe (R-OK)-$529,550
Roy Blunt (R-MO)-$449,864
John Boozman (R-AR)-$149,930
Thad Cochran (R-MS)-$291,905
John Cornyn (R-TX)-$1,134,506
Michael Crapo (R-ID)-$137,006
Ted Cruz (R-TX)-$2,569,810
Mike Enzi (R-WY)-$274,383
Orrin Hatch (R-UT)-$471,250
Mike Lee (R-UT)-$253,415
Mitch McConnell (R-KY)-$1,542,084
Rand Paul (R-KY)-$252,786
David Perdue (R-GA)-$184,250
James Risch (R-ID)-$149,530
Pat Roberts (R-KS)-$417,775
Mike Rounds (R-SD)-$201,900
Tim Scott (R-SC)-$548,276
Richard Shelby (R-AL)-$62,650

Luther Strange (R-AL)-(NA)
Tom Tillis (R-MS)-$263,400
Roger Wicker (R-MI)-$224,000

The Republican Party is no longer recognizable. Those centrist, moderate and conservative elected officials no longer exist, notably Ken Burns, Liz Cheney, Jeffry Lane Flake, Mitt Romney, Adam Kinsinger, David W. Jolly, Mike Gallagher, and others. They have been expunged or left the party on their own out of disgust over radicalized extreme elements and the current Republican Party's inability to govern. This misguided ideology began with the Koch Industries funding of the Tea Party with the "Don't Tread on Me" slogan. On behalf of the Tea Party loonies, Koch Industries advanced their anti-government and anti-regulatory oversight on polluting industries. So now, the Republican Party has been cannibalized, morphing into the MAGA party advocating for an authoritarian dictatorial rule.

Every republican voter should clearly see the ethical and moral underpinnings of your party no longer exist. Consequently, you are a voter without a home. Facing a choice between a twice impeached criminal felon and a pro-democracy, people's rights President in Joe Biden.

This is what Trump's own former cabinet and staff have said about Trump. "He is a F***ing Moron," "Idiot" "An idiot surrounded by clowns," " a dope," "a kindergartner," "a patient in an adult care center," "Empty vessel," "Like an 11-year-old child, a sixth grader," and "a G** D** dumbbell."

Today's inflationary problems, excessive national debt, inaction on border security, women's healthcare rights, curtailment of educational freedoms and infringement on voting rights can be traced back to the Trump Administration. Trump spent $2 Trillion on COVID funding, increased the national debt with $ 1.9 trillion in tax breaks, failed in a trade war, costing over $1,200 for each family, stopped the bipartisan Border Bill from passing in 2024, took away abortion rights, passed over 100 voter suppression laws, and curtailed individual freedoms for LGBTQ+ Americans.

If you want to shake things up in Washington and put America on the right course, then vote the above listed individuals out of office, as they are owned by the fossil fuel industry lock, stock, and barrel. There are 14.5 million other reasons to vote these individuals out of office. That is the number of American families who lost everything, including irreplaceable family photos, heirlooms, homes and joy to floods and fires caused by global warming.

CHAPTER 8

Unfit to Serve

The Most Destructive President in US History

"and if now we cannot end our differences at least we can help make the world safe for diversity for in the final analysis our most basic common link is that we all inhabit the small planet we all breathe the same air we all cherish our children's future and we all are mortal".

—John F. Kennedy

Donald Trump does not care how about how many people suffer for him to be a winner. He uses people, he manipulates people to believe in things that are simply not true. He is a masterful con artist who uses propaganda and incendiary language to gather and control an unsuspecting electorate. Since he has been in the public limelight, he has outright lied, misled, or distorted the facts over 40,000 times. Now he has been twice impeached, four times indicted on ninety-one felony charges, found guilty of rape in E. Jean Carroll civil lawsuit, and in January 2024, was ordered to pay $83.3 million to E. Jean Carroll in a defamation trial.

In February, 2024, Trump's organization was found guilty of fraud by a New York judge and fined $355 million plus accumulating interest. Additionally, he is barred from doing business in New York for a period of three years, and he is required to have a court appointed monitor to oversee day-to-day financial activities for a period of three years. He was party to the fake slate of Trump electors in six swing states, including Georgia where he was booked, had his mug shot taken and is facing Racketeer Influenced and Corrupt Organizations Act (RICO) charges. He used his criminal behavior as a badge of honor to get his followers to send money to finance his legal fees and run a second time for the White House. He cheated construction trade businesses out of their earnings for services rendered, and he had to pay out $25 million in settlements for his failed Trump University. He embezzled money from his charitable foundation and was found guilty. He denied his neighbors living next to his golf course in Balmedie, Aberdeenshire, Scotland access to water for their homes. He engaged in over 4,095 lawsuits before taking office. According to the courts Trump ran his businesses as a criminal organization.

On January 6, 2021, he incited a mob to storm the United States Capitol so he could stay in power by obstructing the certification of the 2020 election. Over 2,000 individuals went into the capital building on January 6th, 2021. They became insurrectionists, terrorists, and common criminals. Five people died as a result and 140 capital police were injured, leaving them with a lifetime of trauma.

On January 7th Vice President Pence certified the 2020 election win for Joe Biden and at 3:41 AM he certified the results from all state electors. Trump's failure to stop the mob actions was a dereliction of his Presidential duty and caused staff and several cabinet members to resign. Education Secretary Betsy DeVos submitted her resignation on January 7, 2021. Mike Mulvaney chief of staff resigned, Elaine Chao Transportation Secretary, Matt Pottinger, deputy national security adviser, Sarah Mathews, former White House deputy press secretary and Stephanie Grisham, former chief of staff to the First Lady and press secretary to the President all resigned.

Trump's incitement earned his supporters years of imprisonment, probation, criminal records and various penalties for acts of sedition. Trump followers are serving as much as 23 years in prison.

So far over 1,400 individuals have been prosecuted in what is largest investigation in the FBI's history. And it is not over. More of Trump's supporters have been identified and are in the pipeline for prosecution. American citizens known as the Sedition Hunters are aiding the FBI to identify perpetrators of their crimes. These sedition hunters use facial recognition software and can identify people by the clothing they wore and other individual markings. Their goal is to identify the remaining fugitives from justice before the statute of limitations runs out at the end of five years in 2026.

Trump does not care about these people. If they lose their freedom and go to prison, if they suffered financially or if their family ties have been obliterated, these followers were just cannon fodder for his personal ambitions.

Surprisingly, a number of those convicted still believe the stolen election myth and that Trump will pardon them once he is president again. Over eighty-one million voters already decided in 2020 not to support Trump. Since then, he has lost more voters because he refused to engage in the peaceful transfer of power. He incited a mob to storm the nation's capital and was derelict in his duties to stop the violence. He lost support from law-and-order voters because of his incendiary rhetoric against judges and our justice system. It is clear he has serious criminal indictments against him. He must not escape punishment since no one is supposed to be above the law. As a result of these court proceedings Trump will lose even more voters.

According to recent polling, 10% of republican voters will not vote for Trump now that he is a convicted felon. Also 22% of Republicans say they will not support Trump in 2024 regardless. The whole episode of mob violence, threats and attacks on election workers, judges, and other Americans could have been avoided if the Republican enablers would have had the courage to tell their electorate the truth. Trump lost! There were no election irregularities or fraud. Biden won the 2020 election honestly. They could have kept repeating it until it sank in. This would have prevented

Trump from trying to stay in power and would have avoided the events that took place on January 6, 2021.

In foreign policy his rude and disrespectful behavior toward world NATO leaders embarrassed the nation. He did get NATO members to pay a greater share of military contributions, which was good. He wrongly abandoned the Paris Climate Agreement and the hard-fought nuclear agreement with Iran. He pulled out of the United Nations Human Rights Council as well, along with seven other international agreements. He abandoned the agreement with Russia to reduce military armaments. He committed the U.S. to leave Afghanistan by May 31, 2021, without a commitment to protect Afghan women's rights to education and public service involvement. He left the Afghanistan government out of the negotiations with the Taliban, undermining their authority. His peace work between Israel and Arab nations was a good step forward, but he failed to relieve the plight of the Palestinian people as part of any agreement.

"The concept of the national interest or American National security are things he does not comprehend," John Bolton, Trump's former national security advisor said. "I do not think Trump can make decisions grounded in national security. His attention span is short, and he does not know much about world history and world affairs. He thinks his personal relationships with foreign leaders, especially the authoritarian ones, are all that matters. Trump could go one way in the morning, a separate way in the afternoon. He does not have the ability to stay consistent for lengthy periods of time. Except for one thing, which is how he looks in the press and in public attention. That is very worrying when you are in a crisis and you need a president who is resolute, who can keep his eyes on the prize and worry about our national security, not his image. I think the hard men of history like Vladimir Putin, Xi Jinping or Kim Jong Un understand what their job is for their respective countries. I do not think Trump understands what the presidency is for ours. I will say having been in the room with him, in meeting those people, having listened in on his phone conversations, I do not think they are friendly with Donald Trump. I think Xi Jinping and Vladimir Putin, Kim Jong Un and others think he is a laughing fool and they're fully prepared to take advantage of him. Trump's self-absorption makes it impossible for him to understand that."

Trump promised Americans the cleanest air and water, stating he is an environmental President. But the truth is, Trump is the most anti-natural environment President in American history beating out Bush and Reagan. His deregulation policies gave the green light to industrial polluters to pollute our waterways, drinking water and the air we breathe. Trump issued an executive order approving the $3.8 billion dollar Keystone pipeline project to carry the Canadian Athabasca tar sands bitumen oil, which has already created an environmental sacrifice zone in the Alberta Province of Canada with massive deforestation, poisoning the water and air, contaminating fish and wildlife and causing death among the Indigenous peoples living downstream. And when this oil is burned it will exasperate the climate crisis.

The Keystone pipeline was to go under the Missouri river near the Standing Rock Sioux tribal lands. Jan Hasselman, a lawyer representing the tribe, said that Trump had unlawfully and arbitrarily sidestepped the findings of the previous administration. "It is an insult to the Standing Rock and all its supporters in Indian country and its continuation of historic pattern of trampling on native rights." The tribe was concerned that the pipeline would contaminate their water source and construction would disturb sacred burial grounds. Hundreds of protestors gathered in opposition to the pipeline. Even though there was barbed wire separating the two parties, the militarized North Dakota law enforcement officers used water cannons in the freezing temperature, teargas, and rubber bullets resulting in mass casualties of injured demonstrators, an unjustified lethal form of violence. In the end the Standing Rock Sioux tribe prevailed.

Trump's cavalier attitude toward the environment which sustains all life is downright evil. He dismantled or rolled back over one hundred environmental regulations that protected Americans from pollution. Trump sold off over thirty-five million acres of public lands to extraction industries. Trump's border wall destroyed miles of the Organ Pipe Cactus National Monument Area and part of the Lower Rio Grande Valley National Wildlife Refuge, and tore up a native American cemetery. He removed from protection and public use 16.6 times more land than Teddy Roosevelt protected with his environmental policies. The Trump Administration rolled over for the fossil fuel, timber, mining, and chemical industries, allowing them to reap billions in regulatory handouts.

According to article in The Guardian by authors Emily Holden and Jimmy Tobias, the Trump administration gave away more public lands for extraction industries, leasing 5.4 million acres, about the size of the State of New Jersey, to oil and gas companies at $2.00 to $16.00 an acre. Drilling on these leases would release 4.1bn metric tons of carbon, equivalent to 1,051 coal plants burning for a year. He decimated the morale of civil service people who were treated like enemies, causing many to resign.

Trumps $1.9 trillion dollar Tax Cut and Jobs Act benefitted Americas wealthiest 1% class. The tax cut was not paid by any offset expense. Benefits fell below expectations with lower job creation numbers and a $1.8 to $2.3 trillion deficit cost. Overall Trump increased the national debt by $7.8 trillion dollars, a 60% increase. Under the Trump administration 2.9 million jobs were lost. He increased the trade deficit by 40.5% and under his watch 3 million people lost their health insurance and the government shutdown for 35 days at the end of 2019.

Trump bungled the Covid 911 response. He failed to safeguard the wellbeing of the American people, his first duty as President of the United States. Upon taking office his administration had been informed by the Homeland Security, Center for Disease Control (CDC), the National Security Council, and the World Health Organization (WHO) about a pandemic response plan playbook by the outgoing Obama administration. Instead of investing to increase medical pandemic supplies and building up a stockpile, he cut the CDC budget by $3.943 billion dollars over a three-year period. Included in those cuts was $200 million for the Predict Monitoring Diseases program established to provide an early warning notification system. He cut science-based staff positions by two thirds in foreign and domestic offices, including Tom Bosset, the Homeland Security Advisor and Tim Ziemer the Director of the National Security Council, two very seasoned professional experts. Trump simply did not take the pandemic seriously, calling it the "China Hoax." Foreign countries were bending the curve on COVID case counts providing good public health information and services, enabling their economies to have partial shutdowns or enable citizens to come out of lookdowns sooner.

Disaster came to America due to lack of preparedness and slow response to the pandemic. Pandemic infections were skyrocketing in the US, leaving America with shortages of ventilators and protection equipment. Trump decided not to take available testing kits from the World Health Organization (WHO) and did not order the US manufacturing of testing kits until months into the pandemic. His daily briefings on the COVID pandemic demonstrated weak leadership. His mishandling of the pandemic created confusion and fell into the realm of ridiculous when he suggested lights and disinfectants could be used to eliminate the virus. He failed to follow the professional advice from the CDC and adhere to science.

America became number one in the world for COVID infections and number one in the world in number of deaths. His malfeasance caused 189,000 Americans to die over a seven-month period. If we could have been testing, tracing, and isolating early on we could have controlled the spread of the disease. An estimated 90% of those deaths could have been avoided, and we would not have had to shut down the economy for so long. Other nations who responded immediately had far fewer deaths.

The American public had to endure economic loss, isolation, suffering, and death. The economy went into free fall requiring a

$2 trillion-dollar pandemic economic relief package. It makes you wonder if preparedness could have avoided adding another $2 trillion to the national debt. Mask and vaccine mandates became a political football, inflated by misinformation money-making enterprises and political gamesmanship. The losers were church goers who did not heed CDC warnings to follow safe protocols. An ABC News analysis of federal data found on average death rates in states that voted for Trump were 38% higher than states that voted for Biden. If you look at the data across America, the highest death counts from COVID 19 were in red states where masking and vaccine rates were the lowest among conservatives and republicans. Despite the pandemic problems, Trump managed to spend one-third of his time in office visiting his golf properties. These golf excursions cost taxpayers $141 million dollars over the term of his Presidency according to state department receipts. He had told voters he would have no time for golf.

On immigration he separated about 4,000 children from their parents. Seven of those children died in US custody. Americans have been led to believe their enemy is the immigrant at the border. The idea that these people are going to erase you or take something from you is a gross misconception. We want these people here. We need these people here. They build a more diverse and vibrant America. They do the jobs most Americans will not do. They contribute economically. They are innovative, hardworking, provide ethnic food options, and raise America's standing in the world. Immigrants will contribute $9 trillion dollars to the US economy over the next ten years. They just need a hand up not a handout. The bible is clear that all people of all races and ethnicities carry the image of God. And no race is superior to another.

Trump's border wall was a mythological political stunt. Mexico did not pay for the border wall. Only eighty-three miles of new barriers were built where none existed before during the Trump Presidency. Before Donald Trump became President, 654 miles of border wall already existed, and some parts needed repair. Americans believed building the border wall was to fulfill a political symbol. At a cost of $15 billion to the American taxpayer because of no bid contracts, it was the most expensive wall ever built, and a wall which could be tunneled under, climbed over, or have a doorway cut through it. The sensible solution would be to deploy more electronic surveillance cameras, motion detectors and employ drones and helicopters to apprehend illegals, and put forth an immigration policy to negate the need for illegal border crossings and migrants accumulating at our Southern border in the first place. Expand and manage the work visa program, allowing foreign workers entry to work jobs Americans refuse to do.

Trumps Trade War with China was a failure. Trade wars are never a promising idea based on historical outcomes. He abandoned Transpacific Partnership Treaty (TPP) that included eleven Asian countries plus the US. This trade coalition functioned as a counterbalance to China's trade pricing dominance. According to the US Farm Bureau TPP would have provided $4 billion in new trade for American farmers. At the time US farm trade was $20 billion built by American farmers based on free trade. These dollars supported local hardware stores, feed stores and farm machinery equipment sales. In the end, US farmers had a trade deficit of $11 billion. The decades of positive trade relations built by the American farmers was crushed by punitive retaliatory reactions. Commodity pricing collapsed, decimating the farming heartland of American. Trump had to pay $28 billion of taxpayer's money to bailout American farmers, since China's retaliatory response was to buy agricultural goods from other countries. This resulted in inflationary costs on goods to American consumers. Trump's blunder cost each US household on average $1,277 dollars for his trade war, inflating everyone's cost of living.

Trump abused and ridiculed our Justice and State Department agencies. The Justice Department had solid evidence that Russia interfered in the US 2016 election. At the Trump-Putin summit press conference in Helsinki, Finland, the question about Russian election interference came up. Trump sided with Putin accepting his denial as opposed to our own intelligence agency. He refused to accept the fact that Russian trolls did interfere in the 2016 election. According to the Mueller report there was no evidence of collusion between the Trump campaign and Russia. However, Russian interference occurred in a "sweeping and systematic fashion." In all, thirty-four individuals and three companies were indicted in the investigation, including Trump associates and campaign officials. The question remains; Could Trump have won the 2016 election without Russian interference?

Trump killed the Obama Clean Power Plan that set limited carbon emissions. He rolled back Obama's' new mileage standards for passenger cars and light trucks, allowing more carbon into the atmosphere. He said he favored the $7,500 tax credit for Americans to buy electric cars but took it out of the final annual federal budget. The EPA's core mission is to "Provide cleaner air, water and land to the American people." Trump promised America would have the cleanest air and water. Among other nations, the US ranks 10th in terms of air quality and 29th overall water quality. Trump appointed Scott Pruitt to head up the Environmental Protection Agency (EPA) a fossil fuel industry insider person in charge of the regulatory process. He pushed aside the EPA professionals with his own agents, shut down the EPA climate reporting website, cut regulations, including allowing coal ash to be disposed of into the environment. Pruitt would later have to resign over abuse of power and extravagant purchases.

Other industry insiders included Secretary of Agriculture Sonny Perdue and Secretary of the Interior, Ryan Zinke. Ryan Zinke had to resign amidst ethics violations. Rex Tillerson, Secretary of State got the boot for calling Trump a "moron." Steve Bannon, Roger Stone, Michael Flynn, Paul Manafort and Michael Cohen were all convicted of crimes. Campaign manager, Corey Lewandowski came from Americans for Prosperity, an organization associated with David and Charles Koch. Trump put fifty of Koch Industry network people into government positions. Trump was only giving lip service to being an environmental advocate. His cabinet picks, with few exceptions, left office because of ethical violations, scandals, or being embarrassed by Trump's language and erratic behavior.

Trump stated that the Republican Party would protect Americans with pre-existing health conditions. At the time of his statement his administration was prosecuting to invalidate Obama Care. If successful, the lawsuit would end protection for 133 million Americans with pre-existing conditions. John McCain saved Obama Care in the Senate and Supreme court justice Roberts recognized Obama Care as being legal.

Trump alienated Black people, Hispanics, and Muslims referring their country of origin as "shit hole countries." He sided with neo-Nazis and KKK members during the march in Charlottesville, Virginia when he said there were, "very fine people on both sides." Trump's First Step Act was a good first step in criminal justice reform to address racial inequities and to lessen punishments for nonviolent drug offenses, even though the reform only applied to federal prisons with the lowest incarcerated numbers. Other states began to adopt reforms including moving away from mandatory sentencing guidelines.

Lifelong republicans and former White House staff voted against Trump. The Lincoln Project has been organized to inform, educate, and stop republicans from voting for Trump, and will continue to do so in the 2024 Presidential election. Reasons given for opposing him were racism, bigotry, sexism, chauvinism, bullying, agitator, morally and mentally unfit, liar, corrupt swindler and lacking moral character.

The Official Results of the 2024 Presidential Greatness Project Expert Survey conducted by Brandon Rottinghaus and Justin S. Vaughn ranked Donald Trump dead last with a score of 10.9 out of 100 points. In other words, the worst President in American history. Additionally, he was ranked as the most divisive President ever. Respondents included both Republican and Democratic social science experts in presidential politics and academic research.

Have a look at the list of regulations which were put in place to protect the public, that the Trump administration reversed. I included the full list so you could comprehend the extent of his nefarious actions. The result is a profound negative impact on public health and America's natural resources and a cause of ballooning healthcare costs. He allowed fossil fuel and mining industries to go into pristine public lands. The New York Times pulled together a list of regulation roll backs. Here are 103 of them. 1) Weakened Obama-era fuel economy and greenhouse standards for passenger cars and light trucks. (2) Revoked California's ability to set stricter tailpipe emissions standards than the federal government. (3) Withdrew the legal justification for an Obama-era rule that limited mercury emissions for coal power plants. (4) He withdrew the United States from the Paris climate agreement, an international plan to avert catastrophic climate change adapted by two hundred countries. (5) Changed the way cost-benefit analyses are conducted under the Clean Air Act making it harder to issue new public health and climate protections. (6) Cancelled a requirement for oil and gas companies to report methane emissions. (7) Withdrew Clinton-era rule designed to limit toxic emissions from major industrial polluters and (8) from fossil fuel companies. he revised a program designed to safeguard communities from increase in pollution from new power plants to make it easier for facilities to avoid emissions regulations. (9) He amended rules that govern how refineries monitor pollution in surrounding communities.

(10) Overturned Obama-era guidance meant to reduce emissions during power plant start-ups, shutdowns, and malfunctions. (11) Weakened oversight on state plans to reduce air pollution in national parks and wilderness areas. (12) Established a minimum pollution threshold at which the EPA can regulate greenhouse gas emissions from stationary sources. (13) Relaxed air pollution regulation for a handful of plants that burn waste coal for electricity. (14) Repealed rules meant to reduce leaking and venting powerful

greenhouse gases know as hydro fluorocarbons from large refrigeration and air conditioning systems. (15) Directed agencies to stop using an Obama-era calculation of the societal cost of carbon, which rule makers used to estimate the long-term economic benefits of reducing carbon dioxide emissions. (16) Issued new guidelines that allowed upwind states to contribute more ozone pollution to downwind states than during the Obama-era. (17) Withdrew guidelines directing federal agencies to include greenhouse gas emissions in environmental reviews.

(18) Revoked an Obama executive order that set a goal of cutting the federal government's greenhouse gas emissions by 40% over 10 years. (19) He lifted the ban on E15, a gasoline blend that would have reduced smog in scorching summer conditions. (20) Changed rules aimed at cutting methane emissions from existing landfills. (21) Withdrew a proposed rule to reduce pollutants sewage treatment plants. (22) Threw out a proposed policy aimed at tightening pollution standards for offshore oil and gas operations requiring improved pollution controls. (23) Amended Obama-era standards for clay ceramic manufacturers. (24) Relaxed Obama-era requirements to monitor and repair leaks at oil and gas facilities, including exempting low-production wells which is a significant source of methane emissions from requirements all together.

(25) Eliminated an Obama-era requirement to capture and store carbon dioxide emissions from new, modified, and reconstructed coal power plants. (26) Proposed a rule limiting the ability of individuals and communities to challenge E.P.A. issued pollution permits. (27) He removed 34,700,000 (million) acres of public lands from environmental protection. (28) Lifted an Obama-era freeze on new coal leases on public lands. (30) He finalized a plan to allow oil and gas development in the Arctic National Wildlife Refuge in Alaska, overturning six decades of protection for the largest remaining stretch of wilderness in the United States. The Trump administration held sales in December, but fortunately had

no takers. (31) He opened more than 18 million acres of land for drilling in the National Petroleum Reserve in Alaska, a vast stretch of land on the Arctic Ocean.

(32) He lifted the Clinton-era ban on logging and road construction in the Tongans National Forest Alaska, one of the largest intact temperate rain forests in the world. (33) He approved the construction of the Dakota Access pipeline less than a mile from the Standing Rock Sioux Reservation. (34) Rescinded water pollution regulations for fracking on federal and Indian Lands. (35) He withdrew a requirement that Gulf oil rig owners prove they can cover the costs of removing rigs once they stop producing. (36) He moved the permitting process for certain projects that cross international borders, such as pipelines, to the office of the president from the State Department, exempting them from environmental review. (37) Changed how the Federal Energy Regulatory Commission considers the indirect effects of greenhouse gas emissions in the environmental review of pipelines. (38) Revoked an Obama-era executive order designed to preserve ocean, coastal and Great Lakes water in favor of a policy focused on energy production and economic growth. (39) Loosened offshore drilling safety regulations implemented by Obama following the 2010 Deepwater Horizon explosion and oil spill, including reduced testing requirements for blowout prevention.

(40) Proposed opening Americas coastal water to offshore oil and gas drilling (but a judge ruled it to be unlawful). (41) Approved the Keystone XL pipeline (but a judge ruled it can't proceed without adequate environmental impact study). (42) Withdrew proposed restrictions on the mining in Bristol Bay, Alaska despite the environmental impact on salmon and other fisheries (but was denied permit). (43) Proposed easing safety regulations for exploratory offshore oil and gas drilling in the Arctic that were developed after the 2013 accident. (44) Proposed weakening the rule that increased royalty payments for oil and gas leases on public lands to prevent companies from underpaying the federal government.

(45) Proposed easing the approval process for oil and gas drilling in national forests by curbing the power of the forest service. (46) Approved the use of seismic air guns for gas and oil exploration in the Atlantic Ocean, which would kill marine life and disrupt fisheries. (Fortunately permitting has been denied to date.)

(47) He weakened the National Environmental Policy Act, one of America most significant environmental laws, to expedite the approval of public infrastructure, such as roads, pipelines, and telecommunication networks. The new rules shorten the time frame for completing environmental studies, limit the types of projects to review, and no longer require federal agencies to account for a project's cumulative effects on the environment, such as climate change. (48) Revoked Obama-era flood standards for federal infrastructure projects that required the government to account for sea level rise and other climate change impacts. (49) Relaxed the environmental review process for federal infrastructure projects.

(50) Overturned an Obama-era guidelines that ended U.S. government financing for new coal plants overseas. (51) Revoked a directive for federal agencies to minimize impacts on water, wildlife, land, and other natural resources when approving development projects. (52) Revoked an Obama executive order promoting climate resilience in the northern Bering Sea region of Alaska, which withdrew local waters from oil and gas leasing and established a tribal advisory council to consult on local environmental issues. (53) Reversed an update to the Bureau of Land management's public land-use planning process. (54) Withdrew an Obama-era order to consider climate change in the management of natural resources in national parks. (55) Restricted most Interior Department environmental studies to one year in length and a maximum of 150 pages, citing a need to reduce paperwork. (56) Withdrew Obama-era Interior Department climate change and conservation policies that the agency said could "burden the development or utilization of domestically produced energy resources." (57) Eliminated the use of an Obama-era planning system designed to

minimize harm from oil and gas activity on sensitive landscapes, such as national parks. (58) Withdrew Obama-era policies designed to maintain or, ideally, improve natural resources affected by federal projects. (59) Revised the environmental review process for Forest Service projects to automatically exempt certain categories of projects. Including those under 2,800 acres.

(60) Ended environmental impact reviews of natural gas export projects at the Department of Energy. (61) Rolled back a 40-year-old interpretation of a policy aimed at protecting migratory birds. The rule imposed fines and other penalties on companies who accidentally kill birds through their actions, including oil spills and toxic pesticide applications. (62) Cut critical habitat for the northern spotted owl by more than three million acres in Washington state, Oregon, and Northern California, opening the land to timber harvesting. (63) Changed the way the Endangered Species Act is applied, making it more difficult to protect wildlife from long-term threats posed by climate change. (64) Weakened critical habitat protection under the Endangered Species Act by making it easier to exclude certain areas, including for public works such as schools and hospitals, and for public lands leased to non-government businesses.

(65) Ended the automatic application of full protections for "threatened: plants and animals, the classification one step below "endangered" in the Endangered Species Act. (66) Relaxed environmental protection for salmon and smelt in California Central Valley (67) Removed the gray wolf from the endangered species act. (68) Overturned a ban on the use of lead ammunitions and fishing tackle on federal lands. (69) Overturned a ban on the hunting of predators in Alaskan wildlife refuges. (70) Reversed the Obama-era rule that barred bait, such as grease-soaked doughnuts, to lure and kill grizzly bears. (71) Amended fishing regulations to loosen restrictions on the harvest of a variety species. (72) Removed restrictions on commercial fishing in a protected marine preserve (73) Proposed revising limits on the number of

endangered marine mammals and sea turtles that can be unintentionally killed or injured with sword-fishing nets in the West Coast. (74) Loosening fishing restrictions intended to reduce by catch of Atlantic Bluefin Tuna.

(75) Overturned a ban on using parts of migratory birds in handcrafts. (76) Opened nine million acres of Western land to oil and gas drilling by weakening habitat protection for the sage grouse. (77) Scaled back pollution protections for certain tributaries and wetlands that were regulated under the Clean Water Act by the Obama administration. (78) Revoked a rule that [prevented coal companies from dumping mining debris into local streams. (79) Weakened a rule aimed to limit toxic discharge from power plants into public waterways. (80) Doubled the time allowed for utilities to remove lead pipes from water systems with elevated levels of lead (81) Extended the lifespan of unlined holding ponds for coal ash waste from power plants. (82) Allowed certain unlined coal ash holding areas to continue to operate even though they have been deemed unsafe. (83) Withdrew a proposed rule requiring groundwater protection for certain uranium mines. (84) Proposed a regulation limiting the scope of an Obama-era rule under which companies had to prove that large deposits of recycled coal ash would not harm the environment. (85) Rejected a proposed ban on chlorpyrifos, a pesticide linked to developmental disabilities in children.

(86) Declined to require industries such as electric power, petroleum, coal products and chemical manufacturing to have enough funds to cover major spills and accidents. (87) Declined to issue a proposed rule that required the hard rock mining industry to prove it could pay to clean up future pollution. (88) Narrowed the scope of a 2016 law mandating safety assessments for potentially toxic chemicals. (89) Reversed the Obama-era rule that required braking system upgrade for high hazard trains hauling flammable liquids like oil and ethanol. (90) Changed safety rules to allow for rail transport for highly flammable liquefied natural gas. (91) Rolled back the requirements of a 2017 rule aimed at improving

safety at sites that use hazardous chemical that was instituted after a chemical plant exploded in Texas. (92) Narrowed pesticide application buffer zones that are intended to protect farm workers and bystanders from accidental exposure. (93) Removed copper filler cake comprised of heavy metals from the hazardous waste list. (94) Limited the scientific and medical research the E.P.A. can use to determine public health regulations.

(95) Limited funding of environmental and community development projects. (96) Repealed an Obama-era regulation that would have doubled the number of light bulbs subject to high energy-efficiency standards. (97) Weakened dishwasher energy efficiency standards. (98) Loosened water and efficiency standards for showerhead and washers and dryers. (99) Changed the process for how the government sets energy efficiency standards for appliances and other equipment. (100) Withdrew the Obama-era efficiency standards for residential furnaces and commercial water heaters that were designed to reduce energy use. (101) finalized a rule that limits 401(k) retirement plans from investing in funds that focus on the environment. (102) Changed a 25-year-old policy to allow coastal replenishments projects to use sand from protected ecosystems. (103) Stopped payments to the Green Climate Fund, a United Nations program to help poorer countries reduce carbon emissions.

Donald Trump is unqualified to serve a second term based on the record of his ruinous first term, his failed economy, his failed handling of COVID, and the fact that he is presently a convicted felon for falsifying business records, convicted of sexual assault, charged with running a criminal organization, participating in an insurrection to stay in power, election money fraud and his professed plans to initiate a dictatorial Presidential rule in a second term. Recently he gained control of the RNC. The first thing he did was purge the organization, getting rid of 66 seasoned personnel. It was not a rational move but a move to get control of the RNC campaign dollars. This is exactly what he would do, if elected, to all agencies and department personnel within the U.S. government—replace them all with inexperienced Trump loyalists, replacing democracy for an authoritarian/fascist/dictatorial rule. Like Putin's Russia, China's Xi Jinping, North Korea Kim Jong Un and Hungary's Victor Orban. Once in office he will advance his presidential power, facilitate more fossil fuel "drill baby drill" destruction. His executive order to fire government public servants would destroy a functioning government creating incomprehensible chaos.

Today, Donald Trump has blocked the Border Patrol Enhancement Act, the most significant plan to end Americas southern border crisis. Why? Because he and his fellow MAGA republicans see an advantage to blame Biden and the democrats for the border crisis, thereby giving an election advantage to Trump. Trump is putting communities and our national security at risk for an extended duration to meet his political objectives. The American people deserve better.

The history books will not be kind to Trump and his political enablers like Speaker of the House Mike Johnson who refused to certify the 2020 election and most recently refused to bring the bi-partisan Border Patrol Enhancement Act approved by 70 Senators up for a vote. He has become one of Trump's minions willing to support the continuation of a border crisis. History will look upon this time with bewilderment, wondering how so many Americans in good conscience could vote for so many individuals of such poor character.

CHAPTER 9

Maniac Master Mind

"Donald Trump is not fit to serve as the president and commander in chief. Trump is a sociopath, sadist, a con artist, a racist, a misogynist, a sexist in general."

—Justin Frank, M.D. psychoanalyst and psychiatrist.

Americans must vote into office individuals of integrity, and intelligence who can articulate good public policy positions. Never vote for someone based on superficial looks, clever slogans, millionaire status, and rhetoric demonizing other people or groups. No one should ever consider voting for anyone who espouses anti-democratic authoritarian rule, or someone who wants to run the country transactionally like a zero-sum business enterprise. American democracy is governed based on our constitution and the rule of law. Our government agencies have a duty and responsibility to provide public benefits to all citizens. Not to profit a few.

Is Donald Trump a pathological liar? Does Trump promote anti-democratic ideals? Does he lack integrity? Does he have a destructive psychological effect on our society? Does he have mental health issues?

The answer to these questions is an unequivocal "yes." He is like a fast-spreading virus having psychological effects on lawmakers and his MAGA base. His poisonous rhetoric channels the words of dictators past and present, like Viktor Orban, Adolf Hitler, and

Mussolini. He works the crowds at his rallies into a propaganda trance clinging to every lie as truth. When MAGA followers are confronted with the truth, they nonetheless mindlessly parrot back his words, as if programmed under his spell in a shared psychosis. Based on his threat to our democracy and his chaotic destructive four years as President, he should never be considered worthy of a second term, particularly since he has told everyone he will rule with an iron fist as an authoritarian dictator.

Wake up and listen to his words. He has told you exactly what he intends to do. In a second term he would unleash his vindictiveness, rage, revenge, anger with ever-increasing velocity. He would tear down from the inside all the agencies and institutions necessary for a functioning democracy. His pathological behavior is a death spiral for everyone and everything around him. His pain and ridicule from his past are entrenched in his psyche. No amount of admiration and loyalty pledges will ever satisfy his internal rage toward anyone who has wronged him, or anyone who said a bad word about him or walked away from his madness. All Americans have watched and listened with bewilderment for years. Most Americans get that there is something wrong with this man because of his sadistic behavior.

Forensic psychologist and author Bandy Lee M.D. wrote three books about Trump's mental illnesses, "The Dangerous Case of Donald Trump," "Profile of a Nation: Trump's Mind, Americas Soul," and "Trumps Mental Health." In her book titled "The Dangerous Case of Donald Trump" Bandy Lee and 37 Psychiatrists and Mental Health experts assess the concern about Trump's psychosis, outlining the clear and present danger posed by a Trump Presidency. "Trump has successfully moved the political discourse into the realm of psychopathology, making the situation even more dangerous."

The future of the planet and humanity are at stake should Trump get a second term. Trump appeals to his wounded followers through the dehumanization of target groups. In Trump's case those include African Americans, Muslims, Women, Hispanics, and

Migrants. Doctor Lee and her colleagues warned of the inevitable rise of mass violence, hate crimes, fear, and suffering.

The likelihood of escalating wars and deaths as a result Trump's anti Iran policies and rhetoric may foretell yet another major and catastrophic war in the Middle East. During Trumps first term the U.S. withdrew from the Intermediate-Range Nuclear Forces Treaty signed in 1987 between Ronald Reagan and Soviet General Secretary Mikhail Gorbachev. The Russian Federation is producing and fielding both "short range" and "intermediate range" land-based ballistic missiles that can carry either nuclear or conventional payloads. The Trump administration was unable to bring Russia into treaty compliance, therefore the U.S. had to abandon the terms of the treaty. As such, it has caused a new nuclear arms race that could end up in the use of nuclear weapons. Atomic scientists have now advanced the doomsday clock to 2 minutes to midnight, the direst proximity to doomsday since 1953 during the thermonuclear arms race between the United States and the Soviet Union.

Today mental health professionals are sounding the alarm, warning the American public just how dangerous Trump is. In a documentary called "Unfit," clinical psychologists discussed Donald Trump's mental issues. John Gardner, a psychologist who taught in the Department of Psychiatry at Johns Hopkins University for 28 years is the founder of "Duty to Warn," an organization of mental health professionals that believe that Donald Trump should be removed from running because he is psychologically unfit.

Erich Seligmann Fromm a social psychologist and psychoanalyst, who escaped the Nazis spent a good part of his life trying to understand the psychology of evil. He formulated a diagnosis he calls malignant narcissism, which has four components: narcissism, paranoia, antisocial personality disorder, and sadism. Erich Seligmann Fromm believes Donald Trump shows signs of this severe personality disorder, "malignant narcissism."

"All his crazy conspiracy theories like Obama's birth certificate, and Ted Cruz's father plus his demonization of legitimate news organizations and of anyone who disagrees with him, these, John Gardner says, "are all signs of paranoia and an antisocial personality disorder, what used to be called psychopathy sociopathy. He is the most documented liar in human history. He violates the rights of other people and exploits them. Sexual assault would be violating the rights of other people. Not paying your bills or defrauding people through Trump University are examples of exploiting other people. He breaks laws, undermines democratic governance, and every Presidential norm. It is part of his personality disorder to break norms and to break laws with lack of remorse. He has no guilt or anxiety about the destructive things that he does. Trump demonstrates sadistic behavior in the way he truly takes pleasure in harming, humiliating, and degrading other human beings."

John Gardner believes mental health professionals have a "duty to warn, to protect society from harm. "The number of people who are at risk, the number of people who could be harmed is not one person. It is hundreds of millions of people. If we did not speak up that would be immoral. I asked this question to whom history will be kinder, those who spoke up during the age when Trump rose to power or those who were silent?"

Author Jennifer Mercieca in her book, "Demagogue for President: The Rhetorical Genius of Donald Trump," explains Trump ran for President both as a dangerous demagogue and as someone who uses rhetoric and polarizing propaganda for his own gain. Mercieca points out the six complementary rhetorical strategies that Donald Trump used consistently throughout his campaign. "One was reification, which is treating people as objects, an animal to dehumanize. Another one is ad baculum which is threats of force or intimidation. The third is ad hominem which is insulting the opposition by name calling. The three rhetorical strategies to bring himself closer to his followers are: The first is ad populum. Trump always praises his people as the best of wisest, the good Americans. Second, he uses paralipsis, which is "I'm not saying, I'm just saying" to ironically say two things at once, allowing him to connect with his audience in a way that they think they know the real Trump and they know what he really thinks. The third thing that he does to bring himself closer to his audience is using American exceptionalism. For him American exceptionalism is America winning. He uses his hero narrative to tell a story of himself promising to make America great again. That he is going to win so easily, and he will win for his people.

"The fact that the nation is struggling with how to control this uncontrollable leader is really the hallmark of a dangerous demagogue. Someone whom we should never give political power to is someone who cannot be controlled, who is unaccountable to the rule of law, to the norms of political discourse. Trump convinced Americans that those norms of political discourse were themselves fraudulent and corrupt. So, he was able to convince his supporters that by breaking those norms he was more democratic than the norms were themselves. He took advantage of the preexisting distrust, polarization, and frustration. Trump's supporters absolutely believe that he is their champion, implementing policies they think are effective or think are good. The appeals he used to convince them he was their champion are themselves anti-democratic. He used rhetoric for compliance gaining, not to persuade, but as a kind of force so people would believe that Donald Trump is on their side. In effect, the rhetorical strategies themselves deny the consent of the governed which is the most anti-democratic thing."

"He has eroded the concept of truth. There is no truth except for what Donald Trump says is true. How do you know what he is saying about the economy is true or what he is saying about the danger of immigrants is true or what he says about anything he says is true? It is a very ingenious strategy, and he has completely eroded truth and made it what he says it is. He is the Alpha and Omega of all knowledge. This denies people the ability to decide for themselves because they do not have crucial information. Trump's audience control strategies are as old as ancient Greece and Rome. Donald Trump did not invent this stuff. It is stuff we have seen before, and we have combatted throughout world history. It is something we should understand because if you want to control the uncontrollable leader you must understand what tricks are employed."

Author Steven Hassan in his book "The Cult of Trump" explains mind control. "The Cult of Trump is hypnotic with his authoritarian rhetoric, long rallies, and chanting. If you chant you feel good about it re-enforcing the cycle of cult identity. Trump overloads his flock with information to get his followers more indoctrinated, getting them to invest their emotions, time, and money while being convinced that it is worth it. Once fully invested, the human tendency is to stick with something even though you know it is a bad idea. Trump also employees glittering generalities, a propaganda device common to politics. It is name calling in reverse. The tactic is to use emotionally appearing phrases strongly associated with high value concepts and beliefs. Slogans that carry conviction without supporting information or reason. Words used to dupe us into accepting and approving of things without examining the evidence carefully. For example, Trump's slogan "Make America Great Again." Great how? Great When? And for whom?"

Trump like other dictators uses fear mongering as one of his most powerful influencers. When fear drives emotions a person sidesteps their frontal cortex, the critical thinking part of the brain, thereby permitting Trump to have quasi mind control over his supporters. All believe what he says is true because he said so and they trust him. He is a dangerous man who is using his unsuspecting followers for their money and to suck energy from his rally attendees to feed his psychosis. It is in your best interest not to attend his rallies, to disconnect from his emails, stop wearing his hats and waving his flags. You should certainly think twice about voting for this criminal jackal.

CHAPTER 10

Stop the Steal and the Big Lie

"A lie can travel halfway around the world while the truth is putting on its shoes."

—Mark Twain

Donald Trump was the candidate of hope and change to his voter base. Trump was responding to voter concerns, resentments, and anger whose cries had long been ignored by the political establishment. His performance on the debate stage was entertaining to say the least, watching him eviscerate his republican opponents. He bragged about being the winner in life, promising to make America Great Again and promising voters would get tired of winning. He was a rich person who had his own money and would not be beholden to anyone. He was the businessperson who was going to shake things up and run the government the right way. Drain the swamp and put America first, as his slogans stated. He promised to stop the flow of immigrants, build the wall, take on the China trade deficit, get out of foreign wars and keep radical Muslim terrorists out of America.

His campaign rallies drew huge crowds. People were excited to hear what he was going to say next. The rally attendees created bonds with one another and often traveled together and communicated with one another between rallies. It was like a big family who shared similar values and beliefs. It was a wonderful experience to participate in these campaign rallies, showing patriotic love for the country. The rallies were something to look forward to. He was viewed to be the best candidate for the Presidency, a tough guy who could take on any adversary and protect the little guy from the big bad wolves—the government and the radical left!

His followers identified with him, idolized, and loved him. Voters trusted him, believing every word about his campaign promises fueling even more loyalty. After all, he told them the one thing they could count on was that he would always tell them the truth. Most followers dismissed any negative comments about his actions. Trump loyalists perceived he was the victim who was constantly under attack from the so-called left wing fake news media, the evil Democrats and the establishment RINO's. Their deep admiration, trust and love blinded these voters from knowing the truth, in part because of inaccurate and misleading information, and because their own victimhood mentality enabled them to relate to Trump in a deep personal way.

Then there was the deliberately deceptive disinformation—Trump's defining the news media like CNN and MSNBC *the enemy of the people*, Trump's way of negating any bad press and keeping his followers from a trustworthy news source, instead using the Fox channel TV commentators to peddle his disinformation. This left Trump followers uninformed and listening to surrogate mouth pieces like Sean Hannity, Tucker Carlson, Laura Ingram, and others who constantly reinforced all kinds of disinformation for the ratings. These individuals have done great harm to this nation along with the advertisers who support the network.

Fox is an entertainment channel with popular TV hosts who are going for sensationalism as news rather than truth. This fact was validated when a judge ruled Tucker Carlson's disinformation was allowed under free speech because Fox is not a news organization but rather an entertainment channel. While one group of voters admired Donald Trump's leadership, the rest of America saw a different man. If you voted for Trump, please bear with me. I believe you can manage the truth and keep an open mind as you read on. For myself, I wished Donald Trump had been the best President ever. Every President begins with that option. We needed a President who was a uniter not a divider. He could have fixed our immigration system without a wall and the separation of parents from their children. He could have been someone who understood foreign trade as opposed to the folly of a trade war. He did not have to reduce America's standing in the world, be a President who gutted public protections from chemical pollution and climate altering pollution, who abandoned the non-nuclear proliferation treaty with Iran, abandoned Americas role in the world to abate Climate destruction, claiming it was a hoax. He didn't have to spend $5 million dollars of US taxpayer money to run a disinformation campaign, or increase the country's national debt by 60%.

While Trump loyalists saw a man of courage and greatness, the majority of America saw a dangerous con man seeking power to rule as an autocrat. By the 2020 election, Trump alienated voters because of his divisive comments, treatment of women and his chaotic legacy. Millions of Americas were put off by his bullying, rudeness and narcistic behavior. Millions of Americans (over 50%) did not want or trust Trump with the Presidency again, based on his performance during his four years in office. No one was out to get him. His impeachments, and all his criminal charges were brought on solely by Donald Trump. About 76% of American voters want the government to do more about climate change. His environmental record was abysmal. There are over 15,000 environmental and wildlife organizations in America, representing millions of voters who would never vote for Trump. Trump alienated voters by his actions and dealings with the fossil fuel industry. Trump sided with the fossil fuel industry and failed to protect the American public from pollution. Going into the election most Americans knew the truth about this man.

The 2020 election had the highest voter turnout in 120 years. By October 3rd, 2019, 52 million American had already voted, taking advantage of early voting due to the Covid Pandemic. The number of registered voters was 206,557,583 (million) according to the US census bureau. Votes counted for the 2020 November election totaled 159,693,981. An increase in voter turnout of 23,021,181 (million) over the 2016 election with voter count of 136,669,276 (million). Joe Biden won with 81,283,098 (million) votes (51.3%) and Donald Trump received 74,222,958 (million) votes (46.8%.). Third-party candidates received 1.9% of the votes cast. Trump did receive more votes than any previous republican presidential candidate in history, but not enough to win in 2020. Biden received 7,060,140 more votes and received 306 electoral college votes versus Trumps 232 electoral college votes, officially certified in all fifty states. Trump only won the 2016 election by 77,744 votes cast in three swing states. Pennsylvania, Michigan, and Wisconsin. Normally a democratic strong hold. Trump lost the popular vote to Hillary Clinton by 2.9 million votes. Trump never had most Americans in support of him.

Coming into the 2020 election Trump's administration's own polling numbers showed that he was behind Presidential candidate Joe Biden. His cover story became, "The only way I can lose is if there is voter election fraud." He continued this false flag statement throughout his Presidential campaign. Lifelong republicans began speaking out and distancing themselves from the man. After four years of his unethical behavior related to hush money payments to a Porn Star, lawsuit settlements with Trump University, Q-Anon conspiracy and white supremacy followers, derogatory comments from past cabinet members, constant chaos with staff turnover, insulting women, disabled persons, etc. His cognitive test comments made people realize he was mentally unstable. Trump also violated the emolument clause of the constitution for using his public office for personal remuneration. According to the Washington Post, Trump lied a total of 30,573 times during his four years in office. This sums up many of the reasons why Trump was not popular with most voters coming into the 2020 election. One could surmise, because of these shortcomings he was already defeated before the vote counting started. Can you see why Trump lost in 2020? He alienated a sizable portion of the American population.

The big election lie was further manufactured by talk show entertainment hosts Shaun Hannity, Laura Ingrams and Tucker Carlson in ratings-driven theatrics. Additionally, disingenuous and misleading comments by 139 republican congressional leaders along with Senators Josh Hawley, Ted Cruz, and Rand Paul.

In her book, "Oath and Honor" Liz Cheney writes about Mike Johnson and his efforts not to certify state electors on January 6th. He read from a letter he planned to issue later that day. "We will vote to sustain objections to slates of electors submitted by states we believe clearly violated the constitution." He claimed that the well-established rules and procedures in four states—Georgia, Michigan, Pennsylvania, and Wisconsin—had been deliberately changed. Of course, Mike Johnson ignored the rulings of the state and federal courts that had rejected those claims in each of those states. Johnson was asserting that Congress, absent any constitutional authority, or legal or factual basis, reject the rulings of the courts and throw out the duly certified electors from each of these states.

Liz Cheney points out, Mike Johnson admitted Congress had no expressed authority or ability to independently prove allegations of fraud in the four subject states, but then asserted that "Since we are convinced the election laws in certain states were changed in an unconstitutional manner, the slates of electors produced under those modified laws are thus unconstitutional."

"Convinced by all we had before us were allegations and legal theories rejected by our nation's courts," Cheney writes, "Even the Trump campaign itself was not convinced. We had no evidence of anything nor any means of evaluating evidence and resolving disputes. Mike repeatedly held himself out as a constitutional lawyer. I know constitutional lawyers including conservative constitutional lawyers. Not even one of them agreed with Mike. Others were equally stunned by Mike Johnson's arguments. Later that night, I heard from Kevin McCarthy's chief counsel, Machalagh Carr. She told me she had made clear to Johnson that his letter was wrong. And that he knew it. She said, she pushed back very strongly when they discussed it that afternoon. Other members pointed out there was an additional flaw in Mike's argument. Why was he objecting only to electors from states that Biden had won? Voting rules in other states, such as Texas and North Carolina had also been changed because of COVID. If this was a violation of the US constitution, why then was Johnson objecting only to states where Trump had been defeated? The question was whether the state legislature had delegated sufficient legal authority to the election officials to make these COVID changes? As one federal District Court judge, and Trump appointee explained, whatever actions the Wisconsin Commission took here, it took under color of authority expressly granted to it by the legislature. Another federal judge also appointed by Donald Trump explained, an action taken by the Georgia Secretary of State is a manifestation of Secretary Raffensberger's statutorily granted authority. It does not override or rewrite state law. Under Mike's theory, simple legal issues about the scope of an official's delegated authority, which had already been resolved by a host of courts, had now become a basis to attempt to throw out the will of the voters and seize the presidency. Mike knew about these and other similar judicial rulings, but he did not care. Because, Liz Cheney points out, Mike Johnson was one of the collaborators to overthrow the 2020 election.

When Chip Roy responded, his message was direct and to the point. "First," he said, "we have no constitutional authority to reject electoral votes. We have one certified slate of electors from each state. The 12th amendment is clear under these circumstances we count. The framers did not intend Congress to select the president. Second, even if you believed Congress did have this constitutional power, the claims about election fraud are false." Chip Roy detailed numerous assertions being made which were patently untrue. He warned that if Republicans were to go down this path, they would be ensuring that Democrats would do the same in every presidential election from there forward. Roy then reminded the members gathered in the capitol visitor center auditorium, "Every one of us but two, had voted to accept the results of our own elections just two days earlier. There was no way we could reject electors who had been chosen in the same election, under the same rules and procedures. If you believe there was a systemic constitutional flaw in how the elections were conducted in these four states, then Republicans elected in those States and those same elections could not legitimately be seated.

"After the 2020 election and the attack on January 6th," Liz Cheney said, "My fellow Republicans wanted me to lie, they wanted me to say the 2020 election was stolen, the attack on January 6th was not a big deal and Donald Trump wasn't dangerous. I had a choice between lying and losing my position in house leadership. No party, no nation, no people can defend and perpetuate a constitutional Republic if they accept leaders who have gone to war with the rule of law, with the democratic process, with the peaceful transfer of power, with the constitution itself."

Liz Cheney was the vice chair of the select committee to investigate the attack on the United States Capitol. She stated in her closing remarks on delivered on Thursday, July 21, 2022, "There was no ambiguity, no nuance. Donald Trump made a purposeful choice to violate his oath of office, to ignore ongoing violence against law enforcement, to threaten our constitutional order. There is no way to excuse that behavior. It was indefensible. . . . Tonight, I say this to my republican colleagues, who are defending the indefensible: there will come a day when Donald Trump is gone, but your dishonor will remain.

I think Vaclav Havel, a Czech statesperson, author, poet, playwright, and dissident best describes the republican party's full embrace of hypocrisy, the art of betrayal, and their guardianship against the truth. Havel concludes, "Individuals need not believe all these mystifications, but they must behave as though they did, or they must at least tolerate them in silence, or get along well with those who collaborate with them. For this reason, however, they must live within a lie. They need not accept the lie. It is enough for them to have accepted their life with it and in it. For by this very fact, individuals confirm the system, fulfill the system, make the system, are the system.' The Republican regime party, if captive to its own lies, must falsify everything. It falsifies the past. It falsifies the present, and it falsifies the future."

It is a profoundly serious matter when the Republican party leadership and members of the Congress continue to support the big lie, all the while knowing that it is a lie, and refuse to tell the truth and refuse to condemn the insurrection that took place on January 6th. I hope that the Trump voters remove their blinders soon, recognize they are being lied to and used for political purposes.

The disinformation narrative culminated in the January 6th insurrection and the attack on our temple of democracy, resulting in the death of five people and injuries to 140 police officers. The violence was in direct response to the former President and the Republican enablers who kept the lie alive, leaving 62% of republican voters still believing that the election was stolen. It is time that our elected officials come clean and tell their voters the truth and stop the deceit. The longer this goes, the angrier the voters will be. Once they realize they have been lied to and used, once they figure out the truth, they will abandon the MAGA Republican party in large numbers.

Following the 2020 election republican candidates running for governor, Senate, House of Representative, state legislatures and Secretary of State were running on the stolen election lie platform. Raising money, purposely misleading the Trump voter base to win their own elections. Claiming the election was stolen was a good vote getter. Peddling a false narrative about nefarious activities such as ballot harvesting, unlawful voting by mail, dead people voting or out of state ballots being brought in, ballots shoved in under the table, dominion voting machines switching Trump votes to Biden and boxes of voting forms dropped off at night.

The truth is, due to the COVID pandemic, several states passed new voting regulations prior to the 2020 election, allowing voting by mail, drop boxes, voting registration changes and how each state counted votes. Therefore, the election was not over on Nov. 3rd because vote counting was still going on. Perfectly normal, nothing unusual about it. This was true in Minnesota, Wisconsin, Michigan, Pennsylvania, Nevada, Arizona, Georgia, North Carolina. Election deniers failed to realize other republican candidates, Governors, Senators, and House of Representatives were on the same ballot as Trump. If fraud existed, then every one of these candidates would have been affected and they would have lost the election as well. No candidate who won claimed fraud in the 2020 election. The only candidate who claimed fraud was the former President who was on the same ballot as everyone else. Logically one can only conclude that the former President is falsely misleading the public.

Every one of these voting fraud allegation complaints by Trump lawyers and voters were fully investigated, reviewed by sixty-one court judges, Secretaries of State, Attorney General Bill Barr (Trump Appointee) and election officials in every battleground state. Election results were recounted twice and some ballots three times. And the results were always the same. Biden won Trump lost.

Trump's appointee Chris Krebs, Under Secretary of the US Department of Homeland Security stated, "The November 3rd election was the most secure in American history." After double checking everything all allegations of fraud were unfounded. We now know that Sidney Powell, Jenna Ellis, Kenneth Chesbro and others have pleaded guilty for their false election fraud claims.

Rudy Giuliani has been disbarred in New York for his false election claims. Giuliani has been ordered to pay $148 million to two Georgia election workers for falsely claiming they engaged in election fraud. Mike Lindell, the pillow entrepreneur, who amplified

Trumps bogus election fraud claims, faces defamation lawsuits from Dominion Voting Systems and Smartmatic for saying their machines were rigged to favor Biden. Mike Lindell continued his election fraud claims challenging anyone who could prove him wrong would win prize money. A judge ordered Mike Lindell to pay $5 million to a man who debunked his false election fraud claims.

The propaganda Fox channel is not capable of reporting real facts. They are misleading the public for higher ratings by telling the audience what they want to hear. CNN is a legitimate news channel with professional journalists reporting the news absent conspiracies. If, for example, Anderson Cooper or other news commentators say something incorrect they point it out and make a public apology. The same goes for MSNBC, Axiom, and other legitimate sources of the real news. I occasionally watch the Fox channel to see what they are telling the public. Fox never covers President Biden's speeches, downplayed the violence on January 6th, said that the FBI was behind the attack on the capital, and peddled the lie that Dominion Voting Machines were rigged to move Trump votes to Biden. Consequently, Fox had to pay $787 million in liable damages for false election claims.

The 2024 Presidential election is about Democracy versus authoritarian rule, women's health rights versus draconian abortion laws, minority voting rights versus voter suppression, public health versus climate altering polluting industries, religious doctrine versus diversity and individual rights.

Trump is a master con artist, a confidence man, a type of defrauder, scammer who manipulated and exploited 46.8% of American voters using modern propaganda techniques into believing his false narratives. He created a fake image of unlimited wealth but does not have the personal cash to pay his multi-million dollar judgments. In a civil case he was found guilty of the rape of E. Jean Carroll, he has been charged with 91 felony indictments, felony charges for the January 6th insurrection attack orchestrated to stay in power, the election fraud case involving Stormy Daniels hush money payment, the $25 million Trump University failure settlement, the Trump Mortgage scam, his serial wife cheating, the access Hollywood tape, his association with Jeffrey Epstein, his blatant racism, casino bankruptcies, failed airline, yacht being repossessed, failed football team, denying water to his golf course neighbors in Scotland and more. A vote for Trump is a way to destroy American democracy and take away personal freedoms.

CHAPTER 11

Rise of Christian Nationalism and Christianity in American Politics

"I never considered a difference of opinion in politics, religion, in philosophy as a cause for withdrawing from a friend."

— Thomas Jefferson

Religion in general can be a sensitive subject to talk and write about. I want to be clear. I am not writing to criticize other people's identity but rather to convey a range of religious and non-religious discussions going on in the public sphere. Today, according to the National Congregational Study Survey, an estimated 380,000 churches exist in the United States. In the U.S. Congress 88% of its members are Christian. The rest of members are either Jewish, Mormon, Muslim, Buddhist, Hindu, Unitarian or unaffiliated. Christian nationalism is affiliated with Christianity. Its primary focus is on the internal politics of society such as legislating civil and criminal laws that reflect its worldview of Christianity. Religion in politics has become a powerful resource to national political leaders as a national movement. It behooves political campaigns to target this national cohesive religious body of Christians. By persuading this bloc of voters that they are the good guys they will capture a substantial percentage of the electorate, provided they parrot a shared worldview, whether it is believed or not.

As of 2023, 65% Americans identify themselves as Christians. The non-Christian religions, Islam, Judaism, Hinduism (oldest religion) and others represent 6%. Adults absent any religious affiliation are about 29%. The highest concentration of Christians is in the Southern states, considered the Bible belt with a figure as high as 86% believing in a God. The first Christian organization was the Catholic Church, which eventually broke into different denominations because of Martin Luther and John Calvin. Christianity is comprised of Eastern and Western theology. In these two divisions there are six branches. Catholicism, Protestantism, Eastern Orthodoxy, Anglicanism, Oriental Orthodoxy and Assyrians. Restorationism is considered the seventh branch. The major Protestant denominations are Adventist, Baptist, Congregationalist, Lutheran, Methodist, Pentecostal, and Presbyterian. All denominations of Christianity believe that Jesus is the son of God and became the sacrificial Lamb of God, believe in the one true and living God. They believe that Jesus Christ is God's beloved son and believe in the Holy Spirit. They believe salvation only comes through Jesus Christ, believe the Bible is the inspired written word of God, and believe Jesus Christ established his church.

The best summation about the rise of Christian Nationalism and its threat to religious freedom and democracy is an article published April 13, 2022, titled "Christian nationalism is Single Biggest Threat to American Religious Freedom." It was authored by Guthrie Graves Fitzsimmons, of the Baptist Joint Committee for Religious Liberty, and Maggie Siddiqi, Senior Director of the Faith and Progressive Policy Institute at the Center for American Progress. "Religious liberty is a fundamental right in the US constitution, yet the meaning of this core American value has come up for debate throughout the nation's history. Today conflicts often arise from Christian nationalism, the anti-democratic notion, that the America is a nation by and for Christians alone. At its core, this idea threatens the principle of the separation of church and state and undermines the Establishment Clause of the First Amendment. It also leads to discrimination and at times violence, against religious minorities and the nonreligious. Christian nationalism is also a contributing ideology in the religious right's misuse of religious liberty as a rationale for circumventing laws and regulations aimed at opposing pluralistic democracy, such as, nondiscrimination protection for LGBTQ+ people, women, persons of color and religious minorities."

In February, 2022, the Center for American Progress, conducted an interview with religious liberty expert Amanda Tyler. She is the executive director of the Baptist Joint Committee for Religious Liberty (BJC) which has a long history of champion religious freedoms. She is the Co-host of the BJC's "Respecting Religion" podcast and a board member of the Center for Faith, Justice, and Reconciliation. She believes the single biggest threat to religious freedom in the United States today is Christian nationalism. "Christian nationalism is antithetical to the constitutional idea that belonging to American Society is not based on what faith one practices or whether someone is religious at all. Christian nationalism is active in American society and manifests itself in harmful ways. The most violent expressions, we saw on January 6th insurrection. The more subtle ones, like state legislative efforts to promote the teaching of the Bible in public schools or to require the posting of "In God We Trust" and the ten commandments in public schools and other public places are also dangerous in that they perpetuate the false narrative that to be a true American one must be Christian. Often a certain type of Christian. Christian nationalism undergirds threats to religious freedom, including anti-Muslim bigotry, anti-Semitism, and government-sponsored religion."

Amanda Tyler states, "Christian nationalism is a political ideology and cultural framework that seeks to merge American and Christian identities. It heavily relies upon a mythological founding of the United States as a "Christian nation," singled out for God's special favor. It is not a religion, but it intersects with Christianity in its use of Christian symbols and language. But the "Christian" in Christian nationalism is more about identity than religion and carries with it assumptions about nativism, white supremacy, authoritarianism, patriarchy, and militarism. The BJC first organized 'Christians Against Christian Nationalism' in July, 2019, when we and our ecumenical partners saw a rising tide of violent Christian nationalism and wanted to organize a resource specifically for Christians to learn more about it and to take a stand against it. As we have learned more, I am convinced Christian nationalism is the single biggest threat to religious freedom today.

"The best way to combat Christian nationalism is to recommit to foundational ideas of religious freedom for all with principles such as:

- People of all faiths have the right and responsibility to engage constructively in the public square.
- One's religious affiliation, or lack thereof, should be irrelevant to a person's standing in the civic community.
- Government should not prefer one religion over another or religion over nonreligion.
- Religious instruction is best left in our houses of worship and other religious institutions.

"We are concerned not only about the threat of Christian nationalism to American democracy but also its threat to Christianity itself. Christian nationalism, which merges political and religious authority, can quickly lead to idolatry and the confusion of allegiance. Patriotism is a laudable value and one that statement signers embrace as well. But when patriotism requires us to sacrifice our religious convictions, then it has ceased to be patriotism and has become nationalism. Christians, particularly white Christians, have a special responsibility and opportunity to understand and dismantle Christian nationalism."

"The BJC has long advocated for religious freedom in Congress and with the executive branch. The Biden administration is keenly aware of religious freedom issues and benefits from the expertise of Melissa Rogers, who serves as the executive director of the White House office of Faith-Based and Neighborhood Partnerships and as senior director for faith public policy on the Domestic Policy Council. In its first year, the Biden administration made good strides in reversing policies of the Trump administration that harmed religious freedom, including the Muslim and African travel ban. One policy that often flies under the radar has to do with the protection of Indigenous sacred lands. Too often, our Indigenous neighbors sacrifice their holy places to satisfy capitalism's greed. BJC is working to protect Chi'chil Bildagoteel, loosely translated as "Oak Flat" in English, which is sacred to the San Carlos Apache and other Western tribes. The current plan is to mine low-grade copper deposits under Chi'chil Bildagoteel, which will not make America more secure or fill American coffers, but it will permanently destroy a sacred sanctuary and encumber already scarce water resources in Arizona. We are continuing to pressure the administration and advocate in Congress for passage of the Save Oak Flat Act."

Tyler goes on to say, "I am a Baptist grounded in theology. The "we" concept of freedom is in the Bible and beautifully expressed by Paul in his ode to freedom in his letter to the Galatians: 'God has called you to a free life. Just make sure you do not use this freedom as an excuse to do whatever you want to do and destroy your freedom. Rather, use your freedom to serve one another in love; that's how freedom grows. For everything we know about God's Word is this single sentence: Love others as you love yourself. That is an act of true freedom.'" (Galatians 5:13 to 14 The Message).

A report, dated January 12, 2023, called, "Discrimination and Barriers to Well-Being: The State of the LGBTQ+ community in 2022," written by Caroline Medina and Lindsay Mahowald covers an interview with Bishop Gene Robinson. He joined the Center for American Progress as a senior fellow and serves as bishop-in-residence at St. Thomas' Parish. In his interview he stated, "This is an exciting time because we are now asking that question about gay, lesbian, bisexual, and transgender people. Could this be yet another time when the church got it wrong about what God's will is? Could this be the time when we admit that we got it wrong? Not that God got it wrong, but we got it wrong, and that God through the Holy Spirit is leading us to the truth about God's, gay, and lesbian, bisexual and transgender children."

Over the last decade religious denominations have been losing members at a rate of one million parishioners a year. White Christian Evangelical fellowship has declined the most by one third. Every day in America nine churches close their doors. Church leadership lost credibility because of their political engagements. Highlighted by recent prostration on the altar of a false prophet-former President Trump and the Republican Party. Past members and potential new members see great hypocrisy. Religious dichotomy between inward faith, outward behavior and language calls into question religious beliefs and creeds, driving people away from participating in organized religion in general, a self-inflected wound. It may be helpful to explore the public's reactions to religious behavior not matching beliefs. Such insights could help understand why people are in a mass exodus from organized religion. These parishioners may not be coming back. Why? Control drama dogma? Denial of science? Religious dogma deviating from core values? Like their ravenous praise for Donald Trump, Evangelical Christians brought the "Serpent" into their houses of worship and now it is destroying their religious faith. Since Donald Trump became President in 2016, four million Christians left their churches.

Evangelicals overwhelmingly voted for Trump because he says aloud, what his voters are thinking. Elevating this morally corrupt individual to being part of God's plan, they think Trumps legal problems are a result of a false notion that the justice department is weaponized. Can Evangelical Christians accept the truth about this man? They invested so much of themselves in him, discrediting their faith over their support of him, causing a split within their church leadership and membership over Christian faith priorities as opposed to the political endorsement of Trump, leaving the Evangelical Christian churches hemorrhaging members. According to a recent Pew poll eleven million Christians left their congregations. Church attendance across all religious denominations has fallen below 50%. The fault line was the shifting attention away from core Christian beliefs and church activities, to political action activities.

The bible does not address the question of abortion. In fact, the word never appears in any translation of the bible. According to the Bible life begins at birth when a baby draws it first breath. The bible defines life as breath. Genesis 2:7, when God "breathed into his nostrils the breath of life; and man became a living soul." The Mosaic law in Exodus 21: -25, directly following the Ten Commandments, makes it clear that an embryo or fetus is not a human being. Is this another matter that the church got wrong, dividing the nation over misguided biblical interpretations unnecessarily? If God moves in mysterious ways, then maybe, just maybe, God's plan is to use abortion to prevent unwanted souls from entering the world. Certain souls may not be ready to be born, needing more time. Creation of life is sacred and a child's conception is to be out of love, so, the child becomes love and joyfully shares that love with the world.

God may not want a woman to bear a child out of violence because it will carry an unsettling energy, disturbing the mother and child throughout their lifetime. And when the child grows up, this child will have problems for his or her entire life. God did not intend for a woman to carry a dead fetus in the womb nor to carry a baby with little chance of survival or one that will have cruel deformities for a lifetime. Shouldn't the mother decide about her pregnancy, given extenuating circumstances without government interference? Isn't it better to respect everyone? Allow others to have the personal freedom to decide for themselves? Rather than infringe on other people's rights, it would be better to focus time and energy on helping others in need—single mothers, the homeless and victims of military conflicts around the world. It is time to stop judging others, and accept everyone out of love and respect. It is time to stop divisive hate rhetoric, division, and pretense for war.

Freedom is having the ability to live, act and speak without constraint. However, freedom ends where freedom starts with another person. You are not free to cause harm to your neighbors or their property. You are not free to use hate speech or threaten another person's life with violence. You are not free to impose your religious beliefs onto another person. You are not free to force anyone to do things they do not want to do. In America, people are to be free from the power of another, free to believe in whatever they want, join any group or religious organization, free to easily and freely start their own churches, free to join cults, free to believe in Q-Anon, flat earth theory, talking snakes or a flying horse drawn chariot ascending to heaven, free to join any number of 45,000 Christian variations in the world. Or any of the two hundred Christian variations in the United States.

Under the US constitution religious freedom is guaranteed. The First Amendment prevents the Federal Government from passing any law that inhibits religious freedom. The First amendment frees any religious denomination, organization, or institution from government interference. The U.S. Constitution states, "Congress shall make no law respecting an establishment of religion or prohibiting the free exercise thereof." A religious person may seek regress from the courts if religious freedom has been infringed upon. Our form of government requires each of us to be respectful of the rights of others as we want them to be respectful of our rights. Under our democracy all Americans are to be free to make life choices. Where to live, career choices, whom to love, reproductive rights and what to believe.

Today 42% of adults in America believe the earth was created by a supreme being and is six thousand years old. And 25% of

Americans believe the sun revolves around the earth. The question often gets asked, How is it that with our high-tech toys and scientific evidence people are stuck in 16th century thinking?

The answer is the literal belief in Holy Scriptures and GEO Concentric Conceit thinking humans are the center of the Universe. The problem arises when religious teaching does not square with reality and young adults figure out the disconnect. Based on an overwhelming amount of scientific evidence humans did not ride or walk among dinosaurs six thousand years ago. Observations teach us that the earth revolves around the sun and dinosaurs roamed the earth sixty-five million years ago.

You can visit the Quarry Wall at Dinosaur National Monument or Dinosaur Ridge west of Denver and walk following the Iguanodon footprints. It is a proven fact. Absolute dating is used to determine a precise age of a fossil by using radiometric dating to measure the decay of isotopes. Faced with such evidence as fossil bones young Christians no longer believe in the creation story. This realization begins to crack the very foundation of certain religious texts and beliefs. Furthermore, they observe the departure from the teaching of Jesus. Love thy neighbor as thyself. Do unto others as you would have them do unto you. The Bible says, take care of the widows, orphans, and foreigners. Jesus did not say love thy neighbor only if he is just like you. He said to love everyone. Jesus made his beliefs clear when he touched the prostitute as he washed her feet. He preached not to judge others, cast the first stone if you are without sin, show compassion and love for everyone. Belief in Jesus means you walk in his footsteps and follow his teachings. Those teachings are being practiced by eight hundred churches in America calling themselves "Sanctuary Churches," providing refuge for foreigners.

Young adults may want to join a Christian church but see a big disconnect between Christian values, words, and actions. If church dogma prevents inclusion, then you are already judging others negatively. Is your religion based on hate battling made-up enemies like evil democrats, socialists, communists, homosexuals, people of color and LGBTQ+ individuals? Does your religious doctrine require your church members to be in a battle, juxtaposed to religious principles and not in keeping with the teachings by Jesus? Is there really a battle to win over the soul of this nation? Could this be another belief that the church got wrong? Do you believe your religious freedom is under attack, or do you want your religious beliefs unlawfully having dominion over this nation?

You may recall the civil servant who refused to issue a marriage license because the couple getting married was gay. Or when a gay couple walked into a bakery to order a wedding cake. The baker realized that two miniature male statuettes would be on top of the cake instead of a man and woman, so the baker refused to make the wedding cake on religious grounds. Why? The baker holds religious beliefs that a marriage is between a man and woman. Therefore, the baker cannot bake the cake. The baker wants freedom of religion to deny service to gay couple? The baker took out a commercial business license that is governed by the laws of the United States. According to those laws a business owner is not allowed to discriminate against people based on sexual orientation or the color of someone's skin. This is a case of religious dogma getting in the way of Christ's teachings. If Jesus was the baker, Jesus would have made the most beautiful wedding cake to honor the love and joy of their union. Why? Because that is where the grace of God resides. In acts of love and in service to others, not in the judgment of others.

CHAPTER 12

Antichrist or Clever Conman?

"I urge you, brothers and sisters, to watch out for those who cause divisions and put obstacles in your way that are contrary to the teaching you have learned. Keep away from them. 18 For such people are not serving our Lord Christ, but their own appetites."

—Biblical text, Romans 16:17

God does move in mysterious ways, right? What if God's plan all along is to evaluate your faith in him over Trump. To see if you will idolize and be submissive to the "Antichrist" or reject him as a false leader. Will you follow the Lord Jesus or the Trumpet man? Church leaders of every denomination had audiences with President Trump. Did they tell him to stop his racist rants, discriminatory policies, and general, divisive rhetoric about the less fortunate? Or stop him from separating children from their parents at the border? Ask him to care about God's creation and protect the planet by maintaining environmental safeguards? To take positive action to address our climate? Or ask him to stop lying to the American public and be an honorable President? It was the Christian voters who wielded the power to get Trump elected in the first place. What, no course correction? No decency? Just Trumpism!

The largest single voting bloc are Evangelical Christians representing about 24% of the electorate who have been blinded by Trump. According to the Pew Research Center 27% of Americans expressed an unfavorable view of Evangelical Christians. Sixty-three percent of Americans believe that churches and other houses of worship should stay out of politics. Seventy-three present say houses of worship should not endorse political candidates during elections. And According to the Pew research two-thirds of Americans say religion should be kept out of government policies. In the public sphere non-Christians hold negative views of evangelicals due to their narrow mindedness, hypocritical, homophobic, misogynistic, racist, and self-righteous attitudes toward LGBTQ+ individuals.

Are Christians delusionally blind to Trumps malfeasance?

Antichrist 45-Bible Prophecy.com podcast identifies fifteen verses in the Holy Bible with specific descriptions that perfectly match Donald J Trump as the Antichrist. His followers use such terms as blameless, a martyr, a victim, and even a savior. And these coincidences keep adding up one after the other, especially since Donald Trump perfectly matches how the Bible describes the Antichrist. How much longer will it be before Trump supporters begin to refer to him as the Lamb of God. Here are those 15 Bible verses about the character traits of the Antichrist, which all point to Donald J Trump as being the man of sin.

1. "The Antichrist will come in his own name and be accepted." John 5:43. In this verse Jesus told the Pharisees, the religious leaders of his day, that although they rejected him, someone else would come in his own name and be accepted. Trump not only arrived on the political scene, having already achieved worldwide fame, versus coming in his own name, but he is now widely beloved throughout Israel, with train stations and town squares named after him and his image appearing on commemorative temple coins alongside King Cyrus. And in a dual fulfillment of

this verse, Christian religious leaders have also accepted Trump as being chosen by God. Being another King Cyrus and even sounded as the savior of America, Trump has come in his own name and Christian evangelicals have fallen head over heels for him."

2. "The Antichrist has the mouth of a lion." Revelation 13:2. Daniel 7 reinforces this verse:4. And the meaning is that the Antichrist will roar like a lion, letting everyone know that he is the king of the beasts. The mouth of the Antichrist is one of his definitive qualities, and just like a lion, it is used to assert his dominance and defend his territory. Trump fulfilled this prophecy the moment he descended the escalator to announce his candidacy. His constant roar has laid claim to being the king of the GOP and left his opponents afraid to say or do anything that might encourage his attacks. In an ironic twist to his prophecy being fulfilled, Trump supporters have embraced him, being portrayed as a lion, blissfully unaware that first Peter 5:8. describes Satan as a lion walking about seeking someone to devour."

3. "The Antichrist is arrogant and magnifies himself above others. Daniel 8:25. Daniel reinforces this verse 11:36, and both verses talk about the Antichrist as being extremely arrogant, someone who was filled with excessive pride about himself and utter contempt for others. And indeed, Trump's arrogance is on full display whenever he speaks. He denigrates others to elevate himself and views himself as superior to those around him. Trump's extreme arrogance is never more obvious than after he's been publicly criticized, as he responds by not only lauding his own accomplishments, including greatly magnifying them, but simultaneously belittling his critics."

4. "The Antichrist is extremely boastful. Daniel 7:8. Revelation 13 also reinforces this verse:5. While the previous verse described the arrogance of the Antichrist, which is his excessive pride, he is also extraordinarily boastful, meaning he incessantly brags about himself. He is constantly saying great things about himself and what he has accomplished or plans to accomplish. Whether or not the things he is bragging about are truthful isn't relevant to him."

5. "The Antichrist will throw truth to the ground. Daniel 8:12. It is not just that the Antichrist will be a pathological liar. But that truth itself holds no value to him. He cast it to the ground as if it were worthless or irrelevant. While Trump's reputation for dishonesty was a known fact for years before even entering politics, he also is adept at manipulating the truth to suit his own needs. Truth itself does not hold any value for him, unless it can be used in a way to promote himself. Astoundingly, despite Trump's casual relationship with the truth, his supporters view him as an honest man who tells it like it is. And yet the reality is that he only embraces what is true when it makes him look good. If it does not then he casts it to the ground. And calls it lies and fake news.

6. The Antichrist will deny the father and his son first by asking who a liar is, but he who denies that Jesus is the Christ. John 2:22 This verse is not only telling us that the Antichrist will deny the father and his son, but that he will do so not out of ignorance, but because he rejects the truth; he is a liar. He will know that Jesus is our savior but will deny him anyway. Trump has been surrounded by Christians and embraced by the evangelical community since 2016, and he is fully aware that Jesus is our savior despite this, and in one of the more stunning admissions by any politician. Trump specifically said that he does not

seek God's forgiveness. This is not only denying a need for the forgiveness of God, but it denies the need for a Savior. Clearly in John 2:22 he is not only lying about Jesus being the Christ, but also denying both the Father and the Son by refusing to seek God's forgiveness.

7. The Antichrist will be a vile person, Daniel 11:21. Contrary to the widespread belief that the Antichrist will be well liked and charismatic, the Bible says he is to be lacking class or decency. He is simply a repulsive, vulgar, and despicable person. Donald Trump uses vulgar language to target others based on their ethnicity, their gender, their intelligence and even their physical appearance. He has made crude comments about his niece and his own daughter, bragged about his sexual exploits with married woman, and his multiple extramarital affairs himself. The way that Trump speaks, and acts is in every sense of the word vile."

8. "The Antichrist will honor the God of forces. Daniel 11:38. This verse is telling us that the Antichrist in his estate shall honor the God of forces with gold, silver, precious stones, and pleasant things. Who is this God of forces? It is a name we all know well. During the fifth century BC, Apollo became known as the Sun God, the symbol of which was often used in ancient battles to represent the God of forces in Revelation 9:11. Trump's Penthouse in Trump Tower includes artwork dedicated to the God Apollo, including a painting on the ceiling called the Aurora Fresco, also known as the Triumph of Apollo, led by the Aurora. Beneath that painting, Trump's estate is adorned with gold, silver, precious stones, and pleasant things. Trump's honors the God of forces."

9. "The Antichrist is connected to Gold Revelation 13:18. This famous verse about the number 666 is points us to

another figure in the Bible, and that figure is King Solomon. The reason it does so is because when Solomon was older, he became a type of Antichrist. As his heart turned away from the Lord and toward Pagan gods. King Solomon was obsessed with gold, having hundreds of Shields made from hammered gold, all his drinking vessels were made of gold. Directly connecting the number 666 in Revelation to Solomon he received 666 talents of gold. He placed the sun God symbolized by gold above all other God's. Trump's own clear obsession with gold, in conjunction with his honoring of the God of forces and his estate, directly parallels King Solomon's obsession with gold. Trump's extreme love of gold is yet another form of honoring Apollo the sun God.

10. "The Antichrist is called the little horn. Daniel 7:81 of the more descriptive names given to the Antichrist is the little horn and early version of our modern trumpet. What so remarkable is that the word trump appears twice in the King James Version of the Bible. First Corinthians 15:52 and first Thessalonians 4:16 and in both verses the word "trump" is an abbreviated form of trumpet which is a little horn. 11. "The Antichrist has a covenant with Daniel. 9:27 One of the more well-known prophecies involving the Antichrist is that he will put together a 7-year agreement between Israel and her neighbors, referred to as the Covenant, which the Antichrist will break the agreement and enter the Third Temple. Trump has called his Mideast Peace Plan the deal of the Century. Trump made that deal back in 2020 as his Abraham Accord. Incidentally, some teach that Daniel 9:27 is a reference to Jesus, but that is impossible because it is a covenant that lasts for only one week, whereas the new covenant is everlasting. One week is telling us that it's the false covenant from the Antichrist."

11. "The antichrist will disguise himself as an angel of light, second Corinthians 11:15 Astoundingly, Christians cast Trump as a force for good portraying him as a light, battling the forces of darkness or standing up for good in the face of evil, which is exactly the kind of deception the Bible warned us about. By disguising themselves as angels of light, Satan and his ministers are mocking Christians and Christianity. This is true since marking his properties with the Trump name all around the world is a mockery of the Christian Cross."

12. "The Antichrist will love money as it is the root of all kinds of evil. First Timothy 6:10. It is noteworthy that the Bible does not make such a proclamation about any other sin as being the root of all kinds of evil—not murder, not lying, not stealing, not lust, nor anything else. It is specifically the love of money that is referred to as the root of all kinds of evil. This love of money can best be defined as greed. This greed for money is the root cause of so much sin, and there is a specific reason why. You see, the love of money and all that money brings is at its heart a desire for the things of this world. And because of that, the love of money is describing the predominant character trait of the Antichrist. He is all about loving money and possessing the things of this world. Interestingly, the man who just so happens to match all the other biblical descriptions about the Antichrist also talked about this subject. "My whole life I have been greedy, greedy, greedy for money. I grabbed all the money I could get. I am so greedy."

13. "The Antichrist is revealed by the falling away, 2nd Thessalonians 2:3 a remarkable and yet often overlooked meaning behind this verse is that the falling away or those that leave the faith, will be tied in with the revealing of the man of sin. In other words, these two events are related

as those who fall away from faith move forward towards the man of sin. Thus, it is the falling away that reveals the Antichrist, as we simply need to look at those who have fallen away from the faith and see who they are gravitating towards. It's not simply a falling away for the sake of leaving the faith, but a falling away from Jesus Christ. And towards the Antichrist that we have seen over the past few years with many Christians and their love affair with Trump. While Trump's vileness would have been repulsive in any other politician, strangely Christians not only embraced him but started talking about him as if he was a man of God. Even worse, Christians now consider Trump as the savior of America, putting him on the same level as Jesus. But to those of us who are watching, their falling away from the faith helps us identify who the Antichrist is, as we simply need to observe who they are embracing instead of Jesus."

14. "The Antichrist has the ultimate ego to call himself God. Second Thessalonians 2:4. In this remarkable verse we are told that the Antichrist will be so full of himself, will magnify himself in his heart to such a degree, and will possess such an out-of-control ego that he will proclaim himself to be God. His proclamation will come in the form of announcing that he is savior of the world, since after all the Antichrist is not only anti Jesus Christ, but he also looks to replace Jesus Christ.

    Who on the world scene who also matches all the verses before this can you picture us ever referring to himself as God or the Savior of humanity? Who else thinks that highly of himself? Who else has that kind of monstrous ego? Does anyone come to mind? In fact, Trump has already referred to himself as the Chosen One, has already thanked those who said he was the second coming of God to Israel, has

> already agreed that only Jesus is better than he is and has already embraced the notion that he is the savior of America. As hard as it is for Christians to accept, the truth is that Donald J Trump perfectly lines up with how the Bible describes the Antichrist."

All pastors, ministers and priests of Christian faith have a duty to warn their parishioners about the unholy alliance with Trump. Trump's power and energy only comes from the adoration and money of his followers. To destroy this Antichrist his followers must simply walk away, and give their money to the Church- not to Trump. Stop attending his propaganda campaign rallies, wearing his hats and carrying his flags. He will melt away like the wicked witch doused with water in the "Wizard of OZ."

CHAPTER 13

Political Ruse

"Facts are threatening to those invested in fraud. When you're dealing with frauds and liars, listen more to what they don't say than what they do."

— DaShanne Stokes

A ruse is more than a lie. A ruse is a false front, an action intended to deceive someone, a distraction trick from what is really going on, a cover story used to hide the truth or disguise illicit or forbidden activities. It involves a more elaborate process of deception than merely making a false claim. Its deception is a cunning concealment of the truth. These acts of deception are specifically created by well-funded think tanks like Americans for Prosperity, the Cato Institute, Donors Trust, and the Heritage Foundation to mention a few.

Millions of Americans have succumbed to the spell binding cacophony of sensationalized rhetoric, causing an abandonment of reasoning and common sense. The first thing for a ruse to work is to create fear. Create an enemy. Blame the justice department, a book to ban, a woke person, the cultural elite, a Tea Party movement. Claim Biden and the democrats are evil doers. It is the other guy! The other guy is different. He does not look like you, speak like you or think like you. He is going to take something from you—your way of life, your identity, your job, or change your community.

Fear is wired in our nervous system and in all humans works like an instinct. Once you become fearful, a distressing emotion becomes aroused, caused by a belief that something dangerous is going to happen. People can become vulnerable to manipulation in mass, even though the facts do not support the belief to be afraid. If you are fearful remember Isaiah 41:10 "Do not be afraid for He is with us. Fear not, for I am with you-be not dismayed-for I am your God; I will strengthen you. I will help you; I will uphold you with my righteous right hand."

Wedge issues are designed to whip up the base to invent fear, anger, and denial to win elections. How can you learn to spot these ruses? To spot a lie? How to avoid becoming a victim? Hear the dog whistle and see it for what it is? Are you able to set aside your pet peeves, firmly held beliefs and be open to new information? Can you spot attacking language often on display in House Committee hearings? Read the parading body movements of an elected official behind a podium, and sense the dishonest energy coupled with facial expressions, voice volume, theatrics, a rehearsed act played out by the person staging the ruse? Are you able to stand back and ask yourself, "Why is he/she saying that? Is the opposite true, regarding the information presented?" Thereby revealing the truth—that the speaker is the culprit projecting onto someone else to cover up his own dishonest words and actions.

Political strategists are masterful at taking a comment, an idea or message and spinning it into a tornado, designed to undermine and hide the truth to advance corporate or political interests over your family's rights, health, and security. A notable example of this is the slogan "Climate Change is a Hoax." The fact is 14.5 million homes have been damaged, or destroyed by fire, floods and mega storms caused by fossil fuel pollution altering the climate. Republicans backed by corporate interests do not want you to make the association, to "connect the dots" between burning fossil fuel and tremendous losses imposed on American families.

It is important to decipher deceptive messages from politicians. Be an independent thinker and don't fall for divisive, deceitful political ruses and give your vote away stupidly. You must see beyond the ranker, demonization, and lying. A good example of this behavior is the recent republican response to President Biden's State of the Union Address on March 7, 2024, during which Republican Senator Katie Britt painted a fearful, bleak but deceptive picture of America. Listen intently to Trump campaign fear-based rally speeches and or republican press conferences for an education on political tactics to reinforce an enemy identity, all based on half-truths or false information knowingly or unwittingly.

The principal ethics code in voting must be for the best candidate regardless of political party affiliation, and your vote must dictate good public policy where the elected official is to steward those policies into law. (see Voter Guide in Chapter 14). Otherwise, we end up with laws and policies that are antithetical to your family's financial health and your quality of life and end up with the highest court in the land, the "Supreme Court" corruptly protecting corporate interests from accountability and restraint. Do not let yourself be influenced by propaganda lies, public relations, front groups, and counterfeit science campaigns who camouflage the truth.

If you hear any of the following political rhetorical phrases, it is a clue you are being manipulated, intellectually insulted, and being told a false narrative. You should be skeptical and scrutinize blame game statements and look for their hidden agendas. Only vote for honest politicians who can articulate good public policy. It is your job to know the difference.

Slogan: The Affordable Care Act (ACA) is government control of your health care!

A good example of deceit and concealment is the Affordable Care Act (ACA) also known as Obama Care. It was all-out attack by the Republican Party on behalf of corporate hospitals and drug and insurance companies because the ACA was taking on the insurance industry monopoly on drug pricing, affordable insurance, and lower healthcare costs in America. The goal of the ACA was to provide insurance to sixty million Americans who had no insurance because they could not afford it, as well as prevent insurance companies from denying coverage based on pre-existing conditions and term limit caps on coverage. The campaign against the ACA was ferocious with over fifty attempts to kill the legislation, effectively spreading fear that it was government takeover of your healthcare. Efforts to kill the ACA continued into the Trump Presidency. Even now on the 2024 campaign trail Trump has boasted to end the ACA.

Why was there such opposition to forcing the insurance providers not to deny insurance coverage for pre-existing conditions? Or have annual financial caps? Or keep college kids on the family's insurance plan until they are 26 years of age? Was it really going to be government-controlled rationing of your healthcare? A form of socialized medicine? Was the government going to get between you and your doctor and, worst of all, set up death panels to deny costly medical procedures? Ironically, death panels did exist within the insurance industry prior to ACA legislation. Sometimes medical doctors, often the same ones, would be given the task of evaluating the necessity of a particular surgical procedure enabling a patient to live longer. Often the decision to decline care would be based on the cost of care. And in some cases, those denied the procedure would die because they were refused the medical procedure.

President Obama recognized the abusive practices being played out against families where insurance claims were regularly being denied. He wanted a public health care option, so families had an alternative to the retail insurance market that was fraught with the denial of claims and was too expensive. Republicans used deceptive tactics to convince the public that the ACA was going to ruin everything. Republicans even forced a shutdown of the government over the ACA. Senator Ted Cruz cost the taxpayers

$60 million because of his showboating theatrics extending the shutdown. This is another example of the sky falling rhetoric to convince voters something bad is taking place. The ACA is now the law of the land. Interestingly none of the fear-mongering rhetoric came true. Did your elected official stand up for your family's needs when it came to the Affordable Care Act? Or did they work to protect corporate interests?

Currently the Biden administration is trying to lower drug prices for the American family. He wants American drug pricing lowered to match veterans', Canadians' and Europeans'. Why can't Americans enjoy the same cost savings benefits? Is it because lobbyists representing the pharmaceutical industry descended into the halls of Congress with $300 million influence dollars to spend, to buy off republican and democrat policy makers. Ask your representative if he or she will advocate for lower prescription drug pricing on your behalf, and improve on the ACA with universal healthcare for all with a focus on disease prevention.

Mark Hyman M.D. in his book the Pegan Diet states, "If you want to lower the total burden of chronic disease, survive another pandemic, save our planet and communities, create a happier, less divided society, we must overhaul the way we grow, produce, distribute, and consume food around the world. We must come together, stop the diet wars, and embrace the healing power of proper nutrition." According to numerous studies 80% of chronic disease in America is preventable with living a healthy life style.

Slogan: Biden's open borders!

Since 1992 the US has quadrupled the number of Border Patrol agents from less than five thousand to 20,000 today. Barrier walls and fences have been erected along portions of the 1,950-mile US-Mexico border. In addition, four hundred Border Patrol agents with high tech surveillance systems, and vehicles were stationed every one hundred yards to prevent illegal crossings.

The Biden Administration in 2022 brought additional resources to the border and the region, scaling up its anti-smuggling operations, expanding coordination support for border cities and non-governmental organizations. These actions are being implemented in close partnership with Mexico and governments across the Western Hemisphere. These steps will help address the most acute challenges at the southern border, but they will not solve all the problems in our immigration system that has been broken for decades. Immigration reform can only happen if republicans in Congress quit blocking the comprehensive immigration reform and border security measures which President Biden proposed on his first day in office. Republicans opposed the additional funds the president had requested for border security and management. Unlike republican officials playing political games and obstructing real solutions to fix our border immigration system, President Biden has a plan and has enacted new enforcement measures.

He imposed new consequences for individuals who attempt to enter unlawfully and increased the use of expedient removal. He announced new measures to encourage individuals to seek orderly and lawful pathways to migration and to expand legal pathways for safe orderly and humane migration. He launched an online appointment portal to reduce overcrowding and wait times at the US port of entries, and increased humanitarian assistance in Mexico and Central America to reduce migration to the United States. He put a plan in place to disrupt criminal smuggling networks and support border communities, taking thousands of smugglers off the streets and countering smuggler misinformation. This operation has led to over 7,300 arrests, forcing criminal smuggling organizations out of business.

Senator John Thune from South Dakota, said in a press conference on January 24, 2024. "We must deal with the national security threat that exists at our southern border. People have been flocking across there now literally through the entire Biden administration. The Biden administration has turned a blind eye and a deaf ear to what is happening down there. We are consistently dealing with threats coming across that border that put the American people at risk, so it must be fixed."

The GOP House of Representatives and Presidential candidate Trump repeat the false claim that President Biden is not acting on the border crisis, that he is not even aware of the scope of the problems at the southern border.

So, let us unpack Senator Thune's statement and examine it for the truth. *People have been flocking across there now literally through the entire Biden administration. The Biden administration has turned a blind eye and a deaf ear to what is happening down there.* The Migration Policy Institute in an article dated January 29, 2024 noted that Biden took 535 immigration actions over his first three years in office, compared to 472 under the Trump administration over his entire four years in office. The Biden Administration's "New Hemisphere Approach" established the Safe Mobility Offices, designed to slow the migrant movement and for countries to accept the returns of their citizens while providing a legal pathway for migration and discouraging illegal migration to the US border. Between May and December of last year DHS conducted over 470,000 removals or returns of those migrants who crossed the southern border without authorization. To respond to the record numbers of migrant encounters, the Biden Administration combined strategies to incentivize arrivals at ports of entry, use stricter enforcement and narrow access to asylum seekers to disincentivize illegal entry.

"Americans are asking themselves now three years into Joe Biden's presidency. Am I better off now than I was three years ago?" Wyoming Republican Senator John Barrasso stated, "Resoundingly the answer is no. People are worse off in terms of their economic and financial security, worse off in terms of border security, worse off in terms of national security. Joe Biden reversed six successful policies that helped secure the border and as the result of those actions we had 8.8 million undocumented immigrants coming into this country. Additionally, Biden and the Democrats passed a massive trillion-dollar reckless spending bill. This triggered the worst inflation in 40 years for which American people are still suffering painful soaring prices every time they go to the grocery store. The American people know they are worse off now than they were three years ago. Joe Biden and the Democrats have squandered the best economy in our lifetime. They have surrendered our southern border to the cartels and the drug dealers, terror suspects and they have empowered our enemies to commit acts of ruthless violence. Under any criteria Joe Biden and the Democrats have made our nation worse because of their leadership and Republicans are committed to putting America back on track."

So much to unpack here! Senator John Anthony Barrasso III's fear-based statements sound like the barbarians are at the gates and the sky is falling. First, the number of migrant encounters since Biden has taken office is 6.3 million migrant encounters not the 8.8 million proposed by Senator John Barrasso. Of these, 2.4 million are in active removal proceedings in immigration court. Under the republican-controlled House, Biden's immigration reform bill has been held up for over a year.

Trump's Presidency did not oversee the greatest economy in our lifetime. When he left the Presidency job losses were at 2,876,000 including 154,000 lost manufacturing jobs, and the unemployment rate was at 6.3% . Today it is 3.7% with fifteen million new jobs created. Trump's economic growth was a negative 3.4%. Under Biden growth in the third quarter of 2023 was plus 5.2%. Under Trump the international trade deficit went up by 40.5%. The federal debt went up by $8 trillion. Handgun production went up by 12.5%, and murder rates were the highest since 1997. Trump's failed trade war and $8 trillion in federal debt drove inflation up along with the supply chain problems during COVID pandemic.

Consumer demand outstripped the supply of goods and drove the costs of goods upward to a 40-year inflation rate of 9.1%. As of March 2024, the inflation rate is just below 3% heading to 2% or lower because of Biden's economic policies, such as the Inflation Reduction Act, The Chips and Science Act, the American Rescue Plan, the Paycheck Protection Plan, the Bankruptcy Extension Relief Act and the Infrastructure Investment and Jobs Act.

The reckless trillion-dollar Biden spending bill was for America's crumbling infrastructure and to address destructive heat-driven weather events. Biden's spending created over 40,000 projects in all fifty states to rebuild bridges, tunnels, roadways, improve our ports, rail, water works and the removal of lead pipes in schools, homes and businesses, The largest portion of spending has been going into red states.

The truth is that President Biden had a border policy plan on day one of his Presidency. But the House for Representatives would not take the bill up to fix the problem. Why? Because if there is a crisis at our southern border, the republicans can gin up their base against Biden and the democrats. The Senate in February, 2024 passed a bipartisan border bill led by Republican Senator James Langford and signed by 70 Senators to fix the problem. Remarkably piercing the sixty Senator filibuster threshold control block. However, Mike Johnson speaker of the House, said it was dead on arrival without even reading it. Why? Because Trump said not to pass the border bill. Republicans do not want the border crisis fixed. They want to campaign on it and not give Biden a win.

Fareed Zakaria of CNN reported the truth about America's robust economy. "Inflation is dropping sharply, real wages are up, and manufacturing employment is experiencing a boom. America's technology sector dominates the world in a way that no country ever has. The value of the top ten US technology stocks is now greater than the value of the entire stock markets of Canada, the UK, France, and Germany combined. The United States has the healthiest demographics of any advanced country, and it takes in around one million legal immigrants a year, which ensures that while Europe and Japan are expected to slowly sink in population, the US will continue to grow."

Slogan: Book banning!

Recent research has found that republican book bans performed very poorly among swing voters. Yet despite this in the past three years legislators in 28 republican-held states have passed 71 bills controlling what teachers and students can say at school. Approximately 4,000 books have been banned by a minority of ignorant people who have overpowered school boards with their fear and infringed on other parents' rights. History tells us that ultimately republicans are right about one thing: school is the ultimate battleground for the outcome of our society. The question is whether we want to indoctrinate kids with hate and white supremacy or whether we want them to develop critical thinking skills.

The solution is not to pull funding and reroute it to unregulated private schools. It is to pay teachers more and direct more dollars towards our public education. Studies conducted over the years have shown that sustained education spending increases improve student outcomes, from test scores to graduation rates to college attendance. Students perform better when more money is spent on public education and the benefits tend to be greatest for lower income students. The republican agenda over the past five decades has been to undermine faith in the public education system. Fear mongering conservatives have falsely claimed liberal teachers have been infiltrating public schools to brainwash kids for years. The republican goal is to extract taxpayer funded vouchers to spend at private for-profit or religious schools.

Slogan: Cancel Culture!

Americans have the right to "vote with their pocketbooks"—intentionally not to do business with companies they feel act or speak in a manner they find unacceptable and to spread the word about firms that discriminate in employment, pollute the air, or make biased statements. Republicans denounce these acts as "Cancel Culture."

Trump insists the goal of Cancel Culture is to hurt businesses and to make decent Americans live in fear of being fired, expelled, shamed, humiliated, and driven from society as we know it."

In an article in McLean Magazine, however, Pamela Palmater counters that the term, "Cancel culture is the dog whistle term used by those in power who do not want to be held accountable for their words and actions—often related to racism, misogyny, homophobia, or the abuse and exploitation of others."

Derek Robertson points out in the "Indianapolis Monthly" that Liz Cheney was stripped of her party position after loudly criticizing Donald Trump's role in the Jan. 6 riots. "If the GOP congresswoman qualifies as a victim of "cancel culture," that begs a long-term overdue question: What meaning does the term have? The haziness about the difference between "cancellation" and plain old criticism or consequences, give it a whiff of sloganeering meaninglessness. "Cancellation can be anything, and therefore nothing."

Slogan: Critical Race Theory (CRT)!

Critical Race theory has been around for decades in academic circles and has been taught in law schools. The purpose behind this education is to understand how racism is embedded and functions in American institutions like our criminal justice system, education system, banking services, labor market, healthcare system, military, voting rights, housing system and avenues for wealth creation. Critical Race Theory looks at all the laws, rules, regulations, and procedures to determine if there are different outcomes based on race.

Critical Race Theory is not taught in elementary schools or high schools. American history is taught, however, in both elementary and high schools, including depictions of the hardships experienced by Native Americans in the United States and America's history of slavery. Republicans have branded this grade school history curriculum as "critical race theory," charging that teaching about race in the classroom will make white kids uncomfortable because of the color of their skin.

Opponents argue that only by understanding and not whitewashing American history, can we comprehend persistent racism and make progress in alleviating the racial disparity that has been institutionalized. Education is a wonderful thing and should not be something to be feared.

Republicans have spun Critical Race Theory into a tornado of false interpretations. As a result, republican-led states have passed laws banning discussions about racism and sexism in the classroom. Republicans have gotten parents so riled up they banned schools from carrying books related to such topics. This is infringing on people's right to free speech and it does a disservice to our children. If we want America to be the best it can be, then we must allow free and open discussions on topics that are uncomfortable for people.

Slogan: Culture Wars!

The term "culture wars" refers to conflicts between groups, especially liberal and conservative groups, that have different cultural ideals, beliefs, or philosophies. In political usage culture wars provoke political polarization as Americans fight to define the nation's cultural values around individual identity, race, sexual orientation, women's rights, and gender. Far-right extremists use stereotyping, labeling LGBTQ+ people as pedophiles or groomers, labeling gay men and Black Americans as dangerous and questioning women's right to abortion.

Slogan: Defund the police!

In 2022, police killed 1,192 people, a record number. One hundred of those killed were unarmed. Black people were three times more likely than white people to be killed even though they were less likely to be armed. The death of George Floyd and Breonna Taylor at the hands of the police sparked the Black Lives Matter movement across the country and "Defund the police!" became a rallying cry in reaction to the police violence against African Americans. This led to republicans charging that the democrats wanted to defund the police.

Democrats instead encouraged the passage of the Justice in Policing Act, creating the broadest law enforcement reforms in generations. Joe Biden and the democrats made it clear that rather than defund the police, they favored making police funding conditional on better training and increasing social services, mental health counseling, and affordable housing.

Slogan: Democrats will force you to give up your gas-powered car & buy an electric vehicle!

There is no legislation or law forcing any person to give up his or her gas-powered car. This rhetoric comes from the fossil fuel propaganda machine. It is true Europe has scheduled a ban on internal combustion vehicles by 2035. The USA will also need to stop manufacturing the internal combustion engine for electric replacement. That is because burning fossil fuels kills people, destroys the planet and its externality cost are not sustainable. It is not because the democrats are out to get you but rather are working to solve a climate crisis problem to protect your home and family from harm.

Slogan: Democrats want to take your guns!

Democrats respect second amendment right to bear arms for protection, as do republicans. No political party seeks to infringe on that right. To solve the gun violence crisis in America, democrats have supported legislation to prevent individuals with mental illness or criminal intent from having access to guns. Over 70% of Americans want common sense gun purchasing rules requiring background checks, a waiting period and red flag laws that alert law enforcement to remove guns from violent individuals. Common sense gun laws would mean fewer mass shootings and in general less gun violence in our communities. The National Rifle Association is spreading lies about new gun laws so gun manufacturers can sell more guns. It is plain old selfish profiteering with total disregard for the victims of gun violence and accidents.

Slogan: Democrats want to take your hamburgers!

Does this at all sound ludicrous to you? It should! What is at play here is that health professionals have been pointing out that too much red meat may be harmful to your health. So, the meat industry went berserk creating a wedge issue blaming liberal democrats. The other contrarian in the mix is environmental folks who are simply pointing out that cattle have an enormous impact on the environment and the climate. There are over one billion cows worldwide. From deforestation in the Amazon for cattle herds, and animal feed crops the impact is significant. It takes nine pounds of feed and 1,847 gallons of water input for one pound of meat output. A 1,200-pound cow yields five hundred pounds of trimmed and deboned meat. Cows use sixty-six thousand gallons of water in their life cycle and need two acres of land equivalent in feed. On two acres you can grow twenty thousand pounds of kale. Kale is rich in vitamins, has 14% more protein than spinach and is good for the immune system. The actual cost of a single hamburger is $4,000 dollars when factoring in all its unpaid external costs. According to the Intergovernmental Panel on Climate Change and Food and Agriculture Organizations of the United Nations-a fully developed cow can emit up to five hundred liters of methane each day, which accounts for approximately 3.7% of all greenhouse gas emissions.

Slogan: Democrats want to take your gas stoves!

Affirming a 1992 summary study on childhood respiratory illnesses, a 2013 peer-reviewed summary report in the International Journal of Epidemiology found children living in a home with a gas stove have a 42% increased risk of experiencing asthma symptoms. Gas stoves pose risks to human health and there are no health-based safety standards for gas stoves. So, the health minded democrat constituents wanted a solution to this problem. The natural gas industry went wild and reached out to their republican proxies to demonize the democrats. All based on early legislative discussions. In January of 2023, 30,000 gas stoves were recalled due to potentially dangerous levels of carbon dioxide emissions. Democrats do not want to take your gas stove. They just want you to know about the health risks associated with gas stoves and use proper ventilation, or buy an electric induction stove which is more efficient, using only one unit of energy to boil a quart of water whereas a gas stove takes three units of energy.

Slogan: Democrats want to take your light bulbs!

On December 20, 2019, the Trump Administration announced that it would block a rule designed to phase out old incandescent bulbs requiring Americans to use energy efficient light bulbs. In announcing the move, the Secretary of Energy Dan Brouillette, who is a former auto lobbyist, said the administration had chosen "to protect consumer choice and ensuring that the American people do not pay the price for unnecessary overregulation from the federal government" The new rule was unnecessary, he said because the innovation and technology are already "increasing the efficiency and affordability of light bulbs without federal government intervention." The real reason this regulation was circumvented by the Trump administration was because it would reduce energy company profits by $14 billion annually. Instead, they claimed it was government overregulation while capturing the $14 billion in consumer savings. Furthermore, incandescent bulbs are costly, a hazard to the environment, poor light quality, have fragility issues, and heating dangers. Democrats do not want to take your light bulbs they are just trying to save you money. If all businesses and homeowners switched out their incandescent bulbs for more energy efficient ones, it would eliminate the need for all coal plants in America and save $500 billion annually in external cost savings related to coal mining, transporting, processing, and burning.

Slogan: Democratic Ideology is responsible for the crime and social decay in our society!

A recent article in the Winchester Star by Catherine Giovannoni illustrates statistics that "point to crime being down in America. The crime wave that started under Donald Trump has been plummeting under Joe Biden. Murder rates rose 30% between 2019 and 2020, the largest single year increase since at least 1905. And under Trump, the rate of aggravated assault rose 12%. The crime wave surge was due to Trumps mishandling of the COVID pandemic as unemployment skyrocketed to 8.05%. Thanks to Joe Biden's programs. . . we have the lowest unemployment rate in the peacetime economy since World War II, and jobs are more plentiful than any time since the 1960s. As a result, crime is down.

In October, the FBI reported that violent crime decreased in 2020 compared to 2021. Homicide rate fell significantly by more than 6% compared to 2021. For the three quarters of 2023, compared to 2022 there have been an 8% decrease in violent crime and a 6% decrease in property crime. Rape is down 15% and robbery has dropped 9%. Analyst Jeff Asher reported that quarterly data shows crime down in big cities, small cities, suburban counties, and rural counties across the board. Red areas continue to experience more crime than blue areas. For example, going back to two thousand, the murder rate in the 25 states that voted for Trump has exceeded the murder rate in the 25 states that voted for Biden. The per capita red state murder rate is 23% higher than blue states. Yes, Magazine recently looked at statistics for white Americans in red states and found that they suffer violent death rates, including from homicide, suicide, firearms, and drunk driving crashes. Far higher than their counterparts in blue states."

It is not the democratic ideology responsible for the increase in crime and social decay. It is the republican officials in red states who have failed their constituents. By not supporting legislation for higher wages so consumer purchasing power is greater than inflation. It is republican representatives who have failed to properly fund public education, pre-school care, elderly care, adequate healthcare services, housing, better jobs, worker rights, alcohol and drug abuse prevention and a safer cleaner environment in which to live. This is why you have a different reality in red states. And voters in those states see what they see and can say things are moving in the wrong direction and they are worse off.

Slogan: Democrats are leftist!

Democrats are called all kind of things. There are democrats who are (leftist) left of center, conservative moderates, liberal, progressive, and socialist. Similarly like the republican party who have in its rank's conservatives, moderates, centrist, and most recently

Donald Trump's non-democratic authoritarian extremist. Democrats are returning to their roots with a vision for America like that of Franklin Roosevelt following the Great Depreciation. The democrats want tax revenues to go to Medicare for all, free public education, a living wage, environmental protection, corporate accountability, voting rights, ending systemic racism, pre-school care, elderly care, women's reproductive rights, mental health services, police reform, criminal justice reform, auditing Pentagon expenditures, and more. In general resources to support public wellbeing across the nation with no one left out.

Slogan: Democrats are socialist!

Democrats recognize that taxpayers' dollars are going into the government coffers. Money earned by all citizens is taxed and paid to the Internal Revenue Service. This money can go to corporate tax schemes, corporate subsidies, bailouts, external costs associated with burning fossil fuels and the like. Or the money can go back to the taxpayers in the form of tax refunds, universal health care, education, food, housing, employment, public works, national security, and things that benefit all Americans, like highways, railways, dams, airports, shipping ports etc. If by "socialism" republicans mean "public benefits," they can call democrats socialists.

Slogan: Democrats are pedophiles!

The notion that democrats are pedophiles started with members of the Q-Anon group who claimed that democrats engaged in a pedophile ring. Marjorie Taylor Greene perpetuated this absurdity on national television and it was thoroughly disproved. It is just another made up fallacy to portray the democratic party as evil people. Unfortunately, some voters believe this nonsense.

Slogan: Demonize LGBTQ+ rights!

A Gallup poll released in 2022 indicated that 7.1% of U.S. adults identify as something other than heterosexual. LGBTQ+ is abbreviation for Lesbian, Gay, Bisexual, Transgender, Queer, Intersex, and Asexual. The additional "+" stands for all the other identities not encompassed in the short acronym. Republican lawmakers have flooded statehouses with hundreds of discriminatory LGBTQ+ laws to cater to their conservative base. ABC News in a report titled, "Republicans use false "pedophilia" claims to attack Democrats," pointed out that Republicans seem to be resurfacing these false stereotypes as a political tool to rile up their base and further marginalize LGBTQ+ people.

"The focus, the experts say, echoes the language used by the far-right conspiracy theory of QAnon, which promulgates the false notion that there is a secret cabal of Satan worshipping pedophile power players who control the government. "It is yet another opportunity to exploit people who are feared, because they actually may obtain power," said Susan Englander, historian at San Francisco State University. "You're going to lie. . .You're going to give [voters] the worst-case scenario regarding what happens if these [progressive] things become normalized." The Parental Rights in Education law, what critics call the "Don't Say Gay" law, spurred debate over whether young children should learn about the LGBTQ+ community in schools, with legislators calling such lessons "indoctrination." Florida, Governor Ron DeSantis signed his bill to ban curriculum mentioning sexual orientation or gender identity in kindergarten through grade three or "in a manner not age-appropriate or developmentally appropriate for students in accordance with state standards. We will make sure parents can send their kids to school to get an education and not indoctrination." In a tweet DeSantis's press secretary, Christina Pushaw claimed that anyone who opposes the Parental Rights in Education bill was "probably a groomer."

According to a March ABC News/Ipos poll, more than six in ten Americans oppose legislation like the Florida bill which would prohibit classroom lessons about sexual orientation or gender identity in elementary school. In Florida, a so-called anti-grooming protests by the far-right extremists and conspiracy theorists took place on the Disney World grounds where protesters falsely accused Disney, the parent company of ABC news, of helping groom children after the company criticized Florida legislators for implementing the so-called "Don't Say Gay" bill. In Michigan, state Republican Senator Lana Theis falsely claimed her Democratic colleague Senator Mallory McMorrow wants to "groom" and "sexualize" kindergarteners and teach "that eight-year-olds are responsible for slavery" in a fundraising e-mail, according to Traverse City ABC affiliate WGTU. In New Jersey, National Republican Congressional Committee claimed Democratic Rep. Tom Malinowski was protecting pedophiles, an accusation he told Yahoo News, was a ploy to rile up their QAnon base. Marjorie Taylor Green of Georgia Republican, who continuously expresses support for QAnon theories, called Democrats "the party of killing babies, grooming, and transitioning children, and pro-pedophile politics. Republicans have made false accusations in a ruse against the LGBTQ+ community to rile up their conservative base of voters. Who are left afraid, confused, and susceptible to manipulation under false pretenses.

Slogan: Energy independence-drill baby drill!

America is already the number one producer of energy in the world, surpassing Saudi Arabia, Russia, China, and Latin America. Today the oil and gas industries have millions of acres under lease and have years if not decades of energy production capabilities. Continued development of oil and gas resources will only lock the world into greater costly climate-altering pollution that the American people cannot afford. Donald Trump and fellow republican politicians use the phrase "Drill Baby Drill" to convince their base that we need more fossil fuel to lower gas prices and save America. In fact, the opposite is true as alternative sources of energy are cheaper for the American consumer.

Slogan: Electric vehicles are expensive and not dependable!

Electric car pricing varies dramatically from under $30,000 to over $100,000. So electric vehicles today are no more expensive the traditional internal combustion vehicles. Electric vehicles have a greater reliability standard because they lack the internal combustion engine with all its moving parts, maintenance, and service requirements. In terms of reliable driving range EV's now have a driving distance range of six hundred miles. And quick charging stations that will recharge a battery in the time it takes to have lunch. However, you must remember to charge your EV at night just like you must remember to buy gas. And just like any long trip by car you must plan for overnight stops. EV vehicles are very dependable despite the negative rhetoric against them. One could surmise that naysayers are beholden to the fossil fuel industry interests, as EV's are a direct threat to gasoline sales.

Slogan: Evil democrats!

In political gamesmanship the democrats must be characterized as evil. If not, then the republicans have nothing. They cannot say, "Gee the Biden economy is great with record unemployment, higher wages, lower crime rates, lower trade deficits and record stock market performance. The democrats have launched over 40,000 infrastructure projects throughout blue and red states with preference going to red states which have been neglected for so long. The democrats are standing up for individual freedoms, voting rights for every American, want to make polluters pay for the degradation of our environment and they stand behind the constitution and Democracy."

So, republicans have to resort to the slogan "evil democrats" to demonize the other party as much as possible.

Slogan: Fake news!

Former U.S. President Donald Trump has repeatedly used the term Fake News to discredit any negative news coverage about him. He has successfully convinced his MAGA followers not to trust mainstream news sources as its all-Fake News, and they are the enemy of the people. In contrast, Washington Post "fact-checkers documented 30,573 false or misleading claims Trump made during his presidency. Commentators and fact-checkers have described the scale of Trump's mendacity as unprecedented in American politics, and the consistency of falsehoods a distinctive part of his business and political identities. Scholarly analysis of Trump's tweets found "significant evidence of an intent to deceive." His language has been characterized as racially charged or racist and as misogynistic. Hopefully soon, MAGA followers will come to see you cannot trust Trump's words. Other republican politicians chime in on Trump's style of deceit. Running on Trumps lies and harsh rhetoric they execute their ruse acts to gain support from the MAGA base of voters.

Slogan: Get rid of the EPA!

The Environmental Protection Agency (EPA) is an agency to protect human and environmental health. Headquartered in Washington, DC, the EPA is responsible for creating standards and laws promoting the health of individuals and the environment. For example, the health benefits from the 1990 Clean Air Act amendments are dramatic; in 2010, over 160,000 lives were saved by the reductions in particulate matter in ozone, and in 2020 it is estimated that 200,000 heart attacks and 17,000,000 lost workdays have been avoided. So why has the EPA been under attack for decades? Most attacks come from politicians representing those polluting and extraction industries. In their talking points they say, "environmental regulations are too expensive, reduce economic growth, hurt international competitiveness, and cause widespread layoffs and plant closures." This rhetoric is a textbook case of ruse language to convince voters the EPA is dangerous and interfering with industry economics.

History demonstrates that when polluting industries are forced to comply with new regulations, they can get the job done, be profitable and competitive. All the while people are protected, and the environment saved from significant health risks. The EPA has regulated auto emissions, banned the use of DDT, cleaned up toxic waste and provided protection of the ozone layer, increased recycling and revitalized inner-city brownfields. EPA achievements have resulted in cleaner air, purer water, and better protected lands.

Slogan: Get rid of the IRS!

The Internal Revenue Service has had its budget cut by more than 15% over the past decade making it near impossible to process tax returns on time and have the staff to review complicated returns thoroughly and in high numbers. Furthermore, the IRS office has been unable to be responsive to taxpayers calling in with questions only answering phone calls 13% of the time. Democrats' solution is to provide more funding which was included in the Inflation Reduction Act for $80 billion over 10 years. The funding would improve computer systems and provide the IRS with adequate staffing to crack down on tax cheats collecting an extra $125 billion to $200 billion over the 10-year period. The good news for taxpayers is that the IRS has been able to hire 5,000 new customer service agents. The IRS backlog has shrunk from 4.7 million unprocessed individual returns to about 400,000. And unprocessed business returns of 3.2 million is down to one million.

The Republican-controlled House has made the Internal Revenue service (IRS) a political target. Republicans have repeatedly falsely claimed that the money from the Inflation Reduction Act will be used to hire 87,000 new agents to weaponize the agency to go after small business owners and middle-class Americans. Some GOP members want to abolish the IRS altogether and replace the entire federal tax code with a national sales tax proposed under their "Fair Tax Act." Which calls for a national sales tax on new goods or services for personal consumption. It must replace the current level of tax revenues so sales tax amounts would have to be set at 30% or more. It would simplify things but has its own challenges. Like people living under the poverty level would have to have some kind of rebate. Then the question of what all is taxed like healthcare. You would still need some kind of agency to oversee collection coordination with states' current sales tax systems as well as states with no current sales taxes at all. Another idea is to have a less complicated, more streamlined tax code dumping tax loopholes for a flat tax solution where everyone pays their fair share.

Slogan: Laissez-faire-smaller government!

Laissez-faire refers to the abstention by governments from interfering in the workings of the free market. It's worth recalling that all great promoters of the market economy, including Adam Smith, John Maynard Keynes, Paul Samuelson, Frederick Hayek, and Milton Friedman, were fully aware of the need for the government to be deeply engaged in public education, road building, scientific discovery, environmental protection, financial regulations, and other activities.

On March 22, 2024, House republican members of the "Freedom Caucus" held a press conference on one hand, condemning size of the $1.2 trillion federal budget and urging the restoration of a small government, but at the same time complaining the government is not doing enough to secure the border, and service the citizens of the country who are buried in debt and crime and drugs and failing schools.

The smaller government theme is driven by corporate interests and peddled by republicans in Congress. You need the size of government that can protect and meet the needs of the American people. After all the government is charged with providing the general welfare of the nation. Laissez-faire is double talk, deceptive, and manipulative.

Slogan: Mask mandates & anti-vaccine politicalization!

In 2023 Drew Weissman and Katalin Kariko won the Nobel Prize in medicine for developing the effective vaccine mRNA to fight COVID-19. It was 95% effective and saved millions of lives. During the COVID-19 pandemic millions of Americans refused to wear a mask or get vaccinated because they did not trust science and saw it as an infringement on their personal freedoms. This created a conflict between individual liberty and the welfare of the whole society.

Shamefully an anti-vaccine, anti-mask sentiment was capitalized on by republican politicians to raise money and win elections. As such there were higher COVID-19 deaths in red states versus blue states. Democrats tended to agree with the science, got vaccinated and wore masks. Over forty-seven million Americans contracted the COVID-19 virus resulting in 1,178,527 deaths. The BMJ, a Global Health Care publisher released a report on seventy-two studies from around the world which concluded that physical distancing, hand washing, and wearing masks reduced the instances of getting the COVID-19 disease by 53%. Face masks limited the transmission of the SARS-CoV-2 virus, preventing respiratory droplets and aerosols from spreading from infected individuals. Because a substantial portion of the US population wore masks it also reduced the death toll from the regular flu season from 60,000 deaths to under 28,000.

Slogan: Overburdensome regulations!

No democrat or republican wants to see government overreaching and being an impediment to economic growth. However, capitalism needs guard rails to protect shareholders and the public from harm. It has been proven repeatedly that corporations will not volunteer to protect the public on their own. They are always trying to maximize profits. So, regulations are the only way to hold unsavory actors in check. Whether it is the fossil fuel industry using our atmosphere as an open sewer and poisoning our water and soil, the extractive industries leaving poisonous mining tailings contaminating drinking water, or the financial markets creating the "Too Big to Fail" conditions—all need to be regulated. Congress passed the Sarbanes Oxley Act in 2002, for example, in direct response to the fraudulent accounting practices and other corporate crimes committed by Enron, World Com, Tyco International and Arthur Anderson executives. The Sarbanes Oxley Act imposed regulatory oversight requiring internal accounting controls with independent auditor reviews, as well as executive accountability for CEO's and CFOs to sign off on their financial statements. Any criminal mischief would be prosecuted. The Act led to the creation of the Public Company Accounting Oversight Board (PCAOB), which set the standards for audit reports.

This is a good example of the need for regulations in corporate America. Still, critics charged that the Act was politically motivated, unfair, and burdensome for executives. Is it not more important to protect workers, investors, and the public at large than to enrich dishonest men? Years of lax lending standards fueled the housing bubble that led to the 2008 wall street fiscal crisis. For three decades the attitude toward wall street was hands off the complicated financial products. Let individual institutions succeed or fail based on their business practices. Regulators, the Securities and Exchange Commission (SEC) and other oversight agencies turned a blind eye. It had allowed the financial system to maneuver to the abyss of total collapse.

Lack of oversight and lack of financial institutional transparency enabled an invisible dark market to run amuck, creating trillions of dollars in toxic asset securities known as "Credit Default Swaps." No one knew the extent of the problem but recognized the financial transactions were interconnected with dozens of banks and other financial institutions and could have a cascading effect. The fear was the depth of the problem would take down the entire world economy. When the real estate bubble triggered a financial meltdown on wall street the US Treasury had to come to the rescue, starting with Bear Sterns, who was unable to meet its financial obligations. It had been bundling subprime mortgages, which became known as toxic assets. The subprime mortgage business became its core business because of the lucrative fees earned.

The Fed bank decided that it had to bail out Bear Sterns to prevent a chain of failures, despite not knowing the size, depth or how widespread the financial problem. When Lehman Brothers was found to have a similar problem, it was denied financial assistance and went into bankruptcy. AIG was in financial trouble and the Feds were forced to act to prop up this insurance behemoth with $180 billion. Government intervention had to cross the Rubicon to save too big to fail banks and other wall street institutions with even more money. Ergo the Troubled Asset Relief Program (Tarp) provided $700 billion bailout funds by the Bush administration before leaving office. Years of neglect in Washington, reckless behavior on Wall Street and evidence ignored by regulators was the underlying cause of the worst monetary crisis in US history.

Regulations are in place to keep corporations from running amok and to protect your family from harm. *Government intervention, over burdensome regulations, the need for smaller government*, are statements used as a smoke screens by corporations.

Slogan: Political correctness!

Political correctness is a term used to describe language, policies or measures that are intended to avoid insulting groups of people because of their ethnicity, sex, gender, or sexual orientation. When the right wing think tanks and conservatives started to use the term as a form of attack, political correctness went from an idea of sensitivity and wisdom to a weapon. Conservatives were able to use the term as a bludgeoning tool with an implication that these policies are extreme or unwarranted. Commentators on the left on the other hand, contend conservatives use the concept of political correctness to divert attention from their discriminatory behavior.

In short, a tool designed to speak without offending anyone has become an attack message between conservatives and liberals.

Slogan: Race baiting!

Ian Haney-Lopez, a constitutional scholar, has written a book entitled *Dog Whistle Politics*. "The notion of *Dog Whistle Politics* is that our political speech is being conducted in code. When you blow a dog whistle, humans cannot hear it, but dogs can. The metaphor is that, in political speech on one level, these coded phrases are silent; and on the other, they are producing strong racial reactions. So, you think about the terms like "illegal alien" or "inner city" or "welfare queen." You cannot find race on the surface, but just below the surface, these coded appeals produce strong reactions.

When Representative Marjorie Taylor Green, Republican of Georgia, stood on the House floor in February, 2024 to announce her proposal to censor the only Somali-born member of Congress, she said she was seeking punishment for "Representative Ilhan Omar of Somalia—I mean Minnesota."

Earlier that same week, Representative Troy Neals, Republican of Texas, called the Black husband of another Democratic woman of color, Representative Cori Bush of Missouri, a "thug." He then said Ms. Bush, who was also Black, had received so many death threats because she was "so loud all the time."

"At a hearing across the capital, Senator Tom Cotton, Republican of Arkansas, grilled the chief executive of TikTok about his nation of origin. Mr. Cotton repeatedly demanded to know whether Mr. Chu, who is from Singapore and of Chinese descent, held a Chinese passport or was a member of the Chinese Communist Party. "No, senator, again, I am Singaporean," Mr. Chu responded with agitation after saying seven times that he was not Chinese. The AAPI Victory Fund, a political action committee supporting Asian American candidates, condemned Mr. Cotton's questioning of Mr. Chu as disgraceful, blatantly racist, and deeply dangerous.

Former President Donald J Trump routinely made bigoted statements during his first campaign for the White House and his presidency. His approach has encouraged Republicans to freely use rhetoric that denigrates people based on ethnicity, religion, or nationality.

Slogan: Rampant crime!

USA reporter Rex Huppke wrote article on December 20, 2023, titled, "Crime in America is down, rudely interfering with the GOP narrative that it is out of control.

A recent Gallup poll found that 63% of Americans described the crime problem in the United States as either extremely or very seriously, up from 54% when last measured in 2021. Only 17% of Americans say the crime problem in their local area is extremely or profoundly serious. "That," Rex Huppke wrote, " shows how effectively we are convincing people that Democratic President Joe Biden has turned the country into a criminal hellscape, even though those same people see no actual evidence to the fact."

Slogan: Renewable energy not dependable, too costly, will not solve our energy problem!

Renewable energy installed power sources represent 21% of Americas power generation. Nuclear energy provides 19% and the rest is with fossil fuels. According to the US Department of Energy (DOE) report wind power accounted for 22% of new electricity capacity installed in the United States in 2022, second only to solar. Representing $12 billion in capital investment and employing more than 125,000 Americans. The report found that transformative tax incentives in President Biden's investing in America agenda-a key pillar of Bidenomics-have led to a significant increase in near term wind deployment forecasts and are helping keep wind power prices competitive with other sources of energy like natural gas. Since taking office, President Biden has launched the most ambitious climate agenda in history, and wind energy both onshore and offshore, will continue to play a significant role in achieving the Biden-Harris Administration's unprecedented energy goals.

"As one of the cheapest energy sources nationwide, wind energy generates enough electricity to power more than forty-three million homes and it's creating good-paying jobs for growing domestic wind energy workforce," says the US Secretary of Energy, Jennifer Granholm. "President Biden is expanding our nation's domestic supply chain, increasing energy security, and growing the wind energy market to drive our clean energy future."

Renewable energy sources like wind and solar are affordable, less expensive than fossil fuel power generation, are very dependable and are solving the energy needs for America. All wind and solar can provide firm power with thermal heat storage or battery back up at grid pricing parity.

Slogan: Socialist democrats!

When republican leadership refers to democrats as socialists, they are referring to their disdain for social programs. No democrat is proposing a communist style end of private ownership. What democrats are supporting is having a safety net for the elderly, those impoverished, mentally ill, disabled, and unemployed. So, we have social security, veterans' benefits, Medicare, Medicaid, the ACA, public education, childcare, elderly care, public works such as the interstate highway and the internet. So, the public and business commerce have good safe roads to travel on. We have a postal service who can deliver mail anywhere in America, even remote rural areas where the cost would normally be prohibitive. It is ironic that republican leadership is opposed to universal healthcare but have no problem creating and supporting corporate socialism with its welfare programs.

Slogan: Tax and spend liberals!

Liberals want wealthy individuals and corporations to pay their fair share. Liberals want to spend to support social security, universal healthcare, public education, abating climate disasters, and safety net services for children and those in need. Today there are twenty-six million Americans without health insurance and 37.9 million Americans living in poverty. The poverty threshold is a family of four earning $29,960 or individuals earning $14,891. Liberals want to increase the minimum wage of $7.25 per hour ($15,080/year) to $15.00 per hour ($31,200/year). This would bring millions of Americans out of poverty and put more dollars into local economies. Liberals want companies to pay higher wages, so taxpayers do not need to subsidize families with food stamps and other assistance.

Slogan: Voter fraud!

The voter fraud myth is used as cover for the Republican legislatures to pass voter suppression laws that are designed to reduce the turnout of minorities who tend to vote democratic. Republicans use fear and intimidation to make it harder for African Americans, immigrants, and poor people to vote.

President Trump's post 2020 election lawsuits about voter fraud have resulted in sixty-four different judges, including Trump appointed judges, rejected his claims of voter fraud. One of Trumps appointed judge writing, "calling an election unfair does not make it so. You need specific allegations and then proof, we have neither here." Trumps own election authorities declared the 2020 presidential vote to be the most secure in American history. Audit after audit, court case after court case have all proven widespread voter fraud did not exist.

Regardless of the facts around election integrity, Republicans continue to push the voter fraud myth to pass voter suppression laws. Fourteen red states have passed twenty-two voting restrictive laws. Each is designed to depress voter turnout.

Slogan: Voter interference confession!

Ken Paxton Texas Attorney General-a republican said on national news that former president Donald Trump would have lost in Texas in the 2020 election if his office had not successfully blocked counties from mailing out 2.4 million ballot applications to all registered voters in Harrison County due to the COVID-19 pandemic. Should Paxton be charged for using his office to interfere with the 2020 election?

The following states vote primarily by mail: Hawaii, Oregon, Utah, Washington, California, Colorado, and most other states provide a no-excuse absentee vote by mail ballot. Voting by mail is a very secure process as signatures are cross referenced and verified.

Plus, all ballots are tracked with a bar code to ensure a singular vote is received and counted. All states should adopt voting by mail to encourage more people to vote in the comfort of their own homes.

Slogan: War on American energy!

Politicians receive campaign funding from the fossil fuel industry, then claim that there is a war on American energy. As of 2022, the oil and gas industry has more than 34,000 leases on public lands covering 23.7 million acres. In public waters, the oil and gas industry has more than 12 million acres under lease. And today America produces more oil and gas that Saudi Arabia and Russia.

What is going on is that renewable energy alternatives are cheaper and non-inflationary. Today more renewable energy projects are being built as opposed to fossil fuel-based power plants. Under the Biden administration new transmission lines are being built to deliver carbon free electricity to your home and business. The fossil fuel industry is entangled in lawsuits for their emissions and disinformation campaigns and facing competition from better, cheaper alternative power generation sources and zero emissions vehicle transportation.

Slogan: War on coal!

The politicians who declare that there is a "war on coal" are receiving campaign dollars from the coal industry. It is not war on coal, but it is a war on the American people. According to a report in the Guardian dated November 23, 2023, "US coal power plants have killed at least 460,000 people in the last two decades." U.S. energy policy should push coal into extinction for the last time, ending its air pollution, land use changes, leaking toxic containment ponds, fly ash and hazardous toxic sludge disposal. And end the coal trains traveling throughout our communities, polluting every mile along the way traveling to power plants for combustion. Some coal trains travel to seaports for export to pollute a foreign land, only to have its pollution come back to us on the trade winds. End mountain top coal mining that destroys rivers and streams. End mercury poisoning of our children, affecting their cognitive learning and neurological problems.

The good news is the US is on track to close half of current coal capacity by 2026. And another 40% of US coal-fired capacity is set to close by the end of 2030. You can vote for politicians who stand with the American people, closing the remaining coal fired plants, putting coal into the dustbin of history, and requiring the coal industry to clean up from its decades long ecological destruction.

Slogan: Weaponization of the Justice Department!

The Department of Justice mission is to uphold the rule of law, to keep our country safe, and to protect civil rights. Republican politicians claim the leftist democrats have done everything possible to take down Trump aided by the liberal media. A Republican House oversight committee was established to investigate the existence of a two-tiered justice system, believing the justice department has been weaponized against Trump and other conservatives. Let us exam the facts.

Both President Biden and Trump were under investigation for their handling of classified documents from the White House after leaving office. In February, 2024, the justice department special counsel Robert Hur found that Joe Biden cooperated with the investigation, never engaged in obstruction of justice nor attempted to hide evidence. As such Robert Hur did not charge Joe Biden for any criminal wrongdoing.

There is, however, a stark difference between Trump and Biden. Trump engaged in obstruction acts and conspired with others to prevent investigators from recovering classified documents. Most notably, after being given multiple chances to return classified documents and avoid prosecution, Mr. Trump did the opposite forcing a search of his home at Mar-a-Lago in Florida. Trump broke the law, has been criminally charged and must go to trial.

Perhaps the real test to determine if there is a two-tier justice system in America is to compare the recent conviction of air national guardsman Jack Douglas Teixeira to Donald Trump's illegal documents case. Teixeira pleaded guilty to six counts of willful retention and transmission of classified information on a social media platform. On March 4, 2024, he was sentenced to 16 years in prison. Trump is charged with 40 counts of willful retention of National Defense information, conspiracy to obstruct justice, withholding a document, corruptly concealing a document, concealing a document in a federal investigation, engaging people in a scheme to conceal and make false statements, as well as sharing classified, secretive information with members of the public. If justice is fair and equitable then Trump should be sentenced to multiple years of prison. If not, then we do have a two-tier justice system.

Slogan: Wokeism!

"Woke" means a state of being aware, to be aware of social problems such as racism and inequality. Wokeness encompasses the need to search for more knowledge, understanding, and truth to challenge injustice. Woke is an adjective derived from the African American Vernacular English. Being "woke" is being informed, educated and conscious of pertinent issues such as social injustice and racial inequalities. More recently woke has come to encompass a broader awareness of sexism, and denial of LGBT rights. Being woke entails recognizing systemic racism around issues of inequality, oppression, and discrimination in society. The concept of being woke is rooted in the pursuit of social justice for racial inequality, police brutality, and cultural reparations. It involves examining power dynamics of oppression and engaging in activism to promote change.

Not everyone approves of the concept. Ron DeSantis, Governor of Florida stated, "Florida is where woke comes to die." The slogan should change to "Florida is the state where freedom goes to die." Due to their draconian laws against CRT, do not say gay ban, book banning, subverting public education, and denying free speech. Republicans are using "FEAR Tactics" to drive these attacks on "woke" education in America today.

Slogan: Deep State!

The conspiracy of the "Deep State" involves the belief that there is a network of bureaucratic career government employees who are secretly manipulating government policy. Most recently the "Q-Anon" conspiracy buffs and supporters of President Trump actively spread false "deep state" propaganda on social media. Trump claimed election fraud and publicly accused employees within the executive branch of actively trying to undermine his agenda. In a second term, President Trump has promised to dismantle the "Deep State" by stripping thousands of federal employees of their civil service protections, allowing them to be fired at will.

A recent retiree from the Foreign Service Institute with years of government service, Nancy McEldowney finds the term "Deep State" both inaccurate and grossly misleading, a dark, conspiratorial term that does not correspond to the reality of knowledgeable, experienced government employees devoted to public service.

Then what is behind belief that there is a deep state at work? Polls indicate a majority of Americans want action on climate change, want women's reproductive rights, automatic voter registration, minimum wage increase to $15 per hour, polluters to pay, fair tax policies, free pre-school and public education, universal health care and a foreign policy that promotes peace in the world. Yet these desires are not being fulfilled. What is going on?

One problem is the legislative process is controlled by minority rule. Mostly republican rural voters have a small population bias voting advantage. For example, Wyoming, with less than 400,000 voters, has two Senators and California with thirty-nine million voters also has two Senators. To get those wonderful things done, Democrats will have to pierce the Republican filibuster threshold of 60 Senators. Which has been blocked by this minority rule in the Senate, because a sizable percentage of conservative rural voters oppose abortion rights, voting rights for all, marriage rights, common sense gun reform and believe climate change is a hoax.

The second factor is right wing extremist groups have captured the Supreme Court with a flood of dark money to the tune of approximately $585 million. Since then, the Supreme Court has abandoned its impartial neutrality position as evidenced by decisions handed down. The Supreme Court has made pretzel moves to comply with corporate objectives by false interpretations of the facts. Senator Sheldon Whitehouse of Rhode Island, stated "The Roberts Court made more than 80 partisan, 5-4 decisions benefiting big Republican donor interests."

The other functionary super political power at work is the Corporate Political Party (CPP) activities which have points of origin in the nineteenth century. But most recently related to the "Powell Memo." In August of 1971 two men got together for lunch. An attorney for Phillip Morris Tobacco named Lewis F. Powell from Virginia and Eugene B. Sydnor, Jr., Chair of the Education Committee of the U.S. Chamber of Commerce. Richard Nixon appointed Lewis P. Powell to the Supreme Court the same year. Eugene Sydnor was looking for help to put together a vision for American business to counteract government authority over business activity, following a slew of corporate financial losses over worker rights, polluting penalties, and more government oversight. So, together they developed a secret strategic plan to assert corporate authority over the legislative process in Washington, DC. The secret pro-corporate plan was known as the "Powell Memo" titled, "Attack on American Free Enterprise System." Their strategy was a long game targeting higher education.

Linda Stamato from Inside Higher Education (IHE) is a policy fellow at the Center for Negotiations and Conflict Resolution at the Edward J. Bloustein School of Planning and Public Policy at Rutgers University. She authored an essay about Powell's manifesto on May 09, 2023. The focus of her essay laid the groundwork for much of what we now see in the efforts to undermine tenure, to prohibit faculty from appearing as expert witnesses to share their professional knowledge in legal proceedings and undermine the autonomy of institutional governing boards, not to mention the explosion of bills and laws emanating from state legislators that would dictate what is to be taught in college and university classrooms. These are but the latest in the multifaceted and unrelenting attacks on higher education, this time focused on what conservatives see as "soft spots," "tenure," "trendy ideologies," "ideological indoctrination," "woke activism," and whatever can be thrown under the umbrella of critical race theory.

These attacks intentionally obscure less visible motive: to support free market ideas and advance corporate interest and those of other powerful market actors. The goal is to influence the institutions that educate future employees and of course, those hired to teach them. Cast in terms of a "cultural war" or "clash of values," the attacks challenge academic freedom and institutional independence and undermine professional expertise while they advanced the "corporate cause" that Powell espoused. Powell's 1971 memo to the US Chamber of Commerce asserted that "the American economic system is under broad attack" and envisioned a comprehensive, coordinated counteroffensive on the part of the American business community in response. Powell singled out "The Campus" as the single most dynamic source of these attacks.

Decidedly critical among his targets, were the courts, as the judiciary may be the most important instrument for social, economic, and political change. Think tanks created alternatives to the professoriate that their creators disdained. As the think tanks—American Enterprise Institute, the Heritage Foundation, the Center for Strategic and International Studies and the Cato Institute -grew, critically placed people were invited to their seminars, conferences and roundtables, and members of the press became more dependent on them. Attacking higher education institutions from outside—or inside, in the case of think tanks affiliated with perceived-to-be-liberal universities such as CSIC with Georgetown and Hoover Institution at Stanford-turned out to be an effective strategy. George Mason University offers another variation on the theme. With $30 million in total donations—$20 million from an anonymous donor and $10 million from the Charles Koch Foundation—its law school became the Antonin Scalia Law School, noted, now, for its focus on law and economics. George Mason also attracted public policy center for Rutgers University, with which a change of name-Mercatus Center-and more Koch Family funding has become a libertarian free market public policy center.

In their 2010 book, Winner-Take-All Politics: How Washington Made the Rich Richer-and Turned Its Back on the Middle Class (Simon and Schuster), political scientists Jacob S. Hacker and Paul Pierson write, "The organizational counterattacks of business in the 1970s was swift and sweeping. A domestic version of Shock and Awe. The number of corporations with public affairs offices in Washington grew from 100 in 1968 to over 500 in 1978. In 1971, only 175 firms had registered lobbyists in Washington, but by 1982, 2,500 did. The number of corporate PACs increased from under 300 in 1976 to over 1,200 by the middle of 1980. On every dimension of corporate political activity, the numbers reveal a dramatic, rapid mobilization of business resources in the mid-1970s.

With the Powell Memo as a backdrop, it may be easier to understand how front and center the Corporate Political Party (CPP) is real and a formative manipulator operating as a loosely organized third political party. They have meetings, raise money, lobby Congress, produce legislative policy agendas, write legislation on state and federal levels, and have their preferred President. Yet they go unobserved like puppeteers in the shadows, "hidden in plain sight".

In his book, "The American Three-Party System" W.D. Wright goes into significant detail exposing the existence of the CPP that is hidden in plain sight. He contends that CPP has overpowered the republican party controlling their legislative policy agenda. W. D. Wright writes, "Corporate Political Party is even more powerful than either of the other two parties shown by the fact that it presently dominates the Republican Party, which is subordinate to it and the national coalition they are in together, and the way it exerts control over and uses a number of Democrats in Congress; and the way it can bring presidents into the fold to have them promote its interests, as it did with Ronald Reagan, George Herbert Walker Bush, Bill Clinton, George W. Bush and Donald Trump, all of whom played a role in letting the corporate elite and their corporation's function essentially unregulated. Which ended up plugging the economy into a serious recession under Reagan and Bush's.

"The American people can no longer remain ignorant about the Corporate Political Party because it engages in the kinds of politics that threatens the integrity and functioning of the national and other governments in this country, as well as the livelihood of Americans. It pushes for the ability to outsource jobs, even having the American people with the aid of presidents and Republicans and Democrats in Congress, help pay the cost of this outsourcing. Because it is trying to destroy or seriously diminish the government safety net that millions of Americans depend on. It is presently using the Republican Party and Democrats in Congress to help it achieve that goal. The CPP wants public money distributed upward to the corporate elite and their institutions, and not downward to make life better for the mass of the American people. It has been able to persuade Americans that government meddling in the corporate economy is a source of their economic and social woes." Most Americans do not understand it, even those who should know better and who should be able to enlighten the American people about the CPP and its constituencies that threaten the US government and the public. W. D. Wright's book was written to try to give the American people a wakeup call about these matters."

The Reagan Presidency institutionalized a "Corporate Fusion Presidential Legacy". While wrongfully claiming "the Government is the problem" The history of where we are today can be traced back to the 40th President. Reagan, Bush, Clinton, Trump where all fusion presidents either knowingly or unwittingly undermining the national government giving over control to corporations to fleece public lands and raid the taxpayer's treasury. Reagan started out by saying the government is the problem and we need to shrink the size of the government. Regan recognized the government is what stands between the citizens and corporate power.

CHAPTER 14

Voter Fraud, Voter Suppression and Minority Rule

"Every government degenerates when trusted to the rulers of the people alone. The people themselves are the only safe depositories."

—Thomas Jefferson

Voter Fraud is a myth. A comprehensive 10-year study, published by the Washington Post found that between 2000 to 2014 there were only thirty-one irregularities out of one billion votes cast. In another study published by the Washington Post found only four instances of voter fraud in the 2016 election. Every state has election security measures in place to deter, detect and protect election infrastructure and processes to ensure election integrity. With all these systems in place and the fact that voting systems are not connected to the Internet, voter fraud is rare or minimal. The election fraud studies found that claims of voter fraud or rigged elections were false rhetoric from the losing party.

Voter suppression, on the other hand, has a long history and persists today. Under the guise of baseless voter fraud claims, republican-held state legislatures have been enacting tactical laws to suppress the vote. In fact, close to four hundred anti-voting bills have been introduced, demonstrating the party's antagonistic stance against people's right to vote. Primarily targeting persons of color who tend to vote democratic, republicans have restricted mail-in voting in dozens of counties, eliminated ballot drop boxes altogether, removed student IDs from the list of acceptable identification, increased residency requirements, enacted an "unelected court system" to undermine Black political power, and introduced laws giving the Secretary of State the power to take over elections.

According to the Brennen Center of Justice, as of January 25th, 2023, at least thirty-two states pre-filed or introduced 150 restrictive voting bills. The legislation is categorized as restrictive if it contains one or more provisions that would make it harder for eligible Americans to register to vote, stay on the voting rolls or vote. The Brennan Center research found the number of voters purged from the voting rolls between 2014 and 2016 was sixteen million, between 2016 and 2018, seventeen million, and between November 2020 and July 2021 over 8.6 million voters were purged. Republican state officials have closed four hundred polling locations in Texas, two hundred polling locations combined in Arizona, Louisiana, Alabama, Mississippi, North Carolina and two hundred and fifty polling locations in South Carolina. All polling locations on college campuses have been closed. Other voter suppression practices include restricting early voting, coordinating disinformation campaigns, voter intimidation, voting time constraints, cumbersome voting registration, voting day obstacles, voting roll purges and new voter ID laws. Interestingly, these practices are unique to republican controlled states.

In contrast, On September 14, 2021, Senator Amy Klobuchar (D-MN) introduced a bill that would expand voter registration (e.g., automatic, and same-day registration) and voting access (e.g., vote-by-mail and early voting), limit removing voters from voter rolls, establish Election Day as a federal holiday and permits former felons to vote. The bill also established a new criminal offense for conduct (or attempted conduct) to corruptly hinder, interfere with, or prevent another person from registering to vote.

Additionally, the bill set forth provisions related to election security, including requiring states to conduct post-election audits for federal elections. The bill outlines criteria for congressional redistricting and prohibits mid-decade redistricting. The bill addressed campaign finances, including the prohibition on campaign spending by foreign nationals, required additional disclosure of campaign-related fundraising and spending, additional disclaimers regarding certain political advertising, and established an alternative campaign funding system for certain federal offices. The bill did not pass. All republicans voted against it.

Rep. Terri Sewell [D-AL-7] introduced the John Lewis Voting Rights Advancement Act on August 17, 2021. The bill would modernize and revitalize the Voting Rights Act of 1965, strengthening legal protections against discriminatory voting policies and practices and establish new criteria for determining which states and political subdivisions must obtain preclearance before changes to voting practices may take effect. Preclearance is the process of receiving preapproval from the Department of Justice (DOJ) or the U.S. District Court for the District of Columbia before making legal changes that would affect voting rights. The bill authorizes the DOJ to require states or political subdivisions to provide certain documents or answers to questions for enforcing voting rights. The bill also outlines factors courts must consider when hearing challenges to voting practices, such as the extent of any history of official voting discrimination in the state or political subdivision. The bill failed in the Senate after it was unable to receive enough votes to invoke cloture.

In Oregon where I live, all voters receive their ballots by mail. Ballots must be received or mailed with a valid post mark by 8p.m. on Election Day. You can drop your ballot in the mail, use any number of drop boxes or take it to an election office. Voters can sit at their kitchen tables in the comfort of their own homes, fill out and sign the ballot. It goes into a special ballot envelope with its own bar code so it can be traced through the mail to election headquarters. You can verify that your ballot has been received and counted. Ballots begin being counted on Election Day. There is no need to wait in line on election day, take time off work, arrange transportation, or hire a babysitter. Voting by mail is by far the best way to vote. No fuss, no muss. No voter fraud because of the signature verification, voter registration card, home address and ballot tracking eliminates any fraud. Let your elected official know that you too would like to vote via mail from the comfort of your own home. It is inclusive and the most democratic way to vote.

There are 90 Congressional seats that are competitive while the other 345 seats are non-competitive. Shockingly you keep seeing poorly performing elected officials continually being reelected, simply because they are politically insulated from being voted out of office regardless of any shameful behavior. Unless republican voters vote their own out of office or more swing voters vote them out of office, we are stuck with them. This problem leaves eighty-nine million Americans without representation because they are considered not to matter as their vote will not count. This is why some politicians are arrogant and dismissive to their constituents. This is an example of the structural conditions that voters must change. Voters should pick their candidates not the other way around. Voters want the power to remove anyone from office who is doing a poor job or aligning with special interests over public good. This election control has led to doubt about our democracy, anger, and resentment. Voters want their voices heard and elected officials responsive to their rights.

The winner of Presidential elections is based on a candidate receiving 270 electoral college votes out of 538. It is not based on the candidate who receives the greatest number of popular votes. In the 2000 Bush versus Gore presidential campaign; Bush won because he received 371 electoral college votes even though he lost the popular vote. And in the 2016 Presidential election of Trump versus Clinton, Trump won with 304 electoral college votes but lost the popular vote to Hillary Clinton by 2.9 million. Here lies the fundamental flaw with the electoral college system. Because the Presidential election comes down to swing states, states that could swing to either Democratic or Republican candidates, political parties often spend a disproportionate amount of time and campaign resources on winning these states, often ignoring other voters in less contested states.

The swing states in the 2016 presidential election were Arizona, Georgia, Michigan, Pennsylvania, and Wisconsin. Trump won Clintons three blue states, Michigan, Wisconsin, and Pennsylvania by 77,744 votes. The tight margin in races indicate that a state could be won by either party often won by a margin of three points or less. The 2020 presidential election came down to five swing states Biden flipped: Arizona, Georgia, Michigan, Pennsylvania, and Wisconsin. Biden's election win came down to just over 44,000 votes. Even though he won the popular vote by 7.1 million votes. The 2024 presidential election will come down to a few battleground states. There are two pathways to ensure all people's vote counts equally. One is to abolish the electoral college voting system, which is exceedingly difficult to do because it requires a constitutional amendment, which requires a two-thirds vote in both Houses of Congress, followed by ratification of 3/4ths of the states. Near impossible to do in our current political climate.

The other way forward is for states to join the national popular vote Interstate compact. This will guarantee the presidency to the candidate who receives the most popular votes nationwide without the constitutional amendment. What is required is for each state to pledge their number of electors assigned under the electoral college to a "national popular vote Interstate compact," aggregating votes from states to reach a total of 270 electoral votes or more and agree to award all their electoral votes to the presidential candidate who wins the national popular vote. This idea already has traction with 17 states and the District of Columbia. They include Washington,

Maryland, New Jersey, Illinois, Hawaii. Massachusetts, Vermont, California, Rhode Island, New York, Connecticut, Colorado, Delaware, New Mexico, Oregon, Minnesota and West Virginia. Those pending states to become signatories to the compact are Nevada, Arizona, Kansas, Wisconsin, Michigan, Main, West Virginia, North and South Carolina representing 88 Electoral votes for a total of 293.

Hopefully, America will never again elect a president who loses the national popular vote. And no longer will 80% of voters be disenfranchised or the election process be vulnerable to manipulation by just a few thousand votes. Instead, the national popular vote interstate compact represents millions of votes, preventing manipulation and every person's vote to be counted equally.

The Republican party today poses an extremely dangerous threat to American Democracy because they are protecting their power of minority rule in the Senate and republican-held state legislatures, made possible through gerrymandering in their favor and their control over more rural states with voting advantage. For example, Wyoming with a population of 581,000 has two Senators and California with a population of thirty-nine million also has just two Senators. A voter in Wyoming has seventy times more influence in the US Senate than a voter in California. This creates a rural state bias and a system of partisan minority rule.

In their book, "Tyranny of the Minority," Steven Levitsky and Daniel Ziblatt charge that America risks descending into authoritarian minority rule, an unusual and undemocratic situation in which a party that wins fewer votes than its rivals nevertheless maintains control over key levers of political power.

That is in part due to the Electoral College, which except for Maine and Nebraska, allocates votes in a winner take all manner, turning the loser of the national popular vote into the winner in an election.

Between 1992 and 2020, the Republican Party has lost the popular vote in every presidential election except 2004, and yet the Republican Party won the presidency three times, allowing the party to occupy the presidency for twelve of those 28 years.

In the US Senate the GOP's dominance in low population states allows it to control the US Senate without winning national popular majorities. The Democrats have won an overall popular majority for the Senate in every six-year cycle since 1996 to 2002. And yet, the Republicans controlled the Senate for most of this time. At no time during the 21st century have Senate Republicans represented a majority of the US population. Based on states' populations, Senate Democrats have continuously represented more Americans since 1999.

Given the nature of the Electoral College and the Senate, Supreme Court justices may be nominated by presidents who lost the popular vote and confirmed by Senate majorities that represent only a minority of Americans. Four of the nine current Supreme Court justices -Clarence Thomas, Neil Gorsuch, Brett Kavanaugh and Amy Coney Barrett—were confirmed by a Senate Majority that collectively won a minority of the popular vote in Senate elections, and three of them—Gorsuch, Kavanaugh and Coney Barrett—were also nominated by a president who lost the popular vote.

Steven Levitsky and Daniel Ziblatt points out how the democratic voters are concentrated in metropolitan centers, whereas Republican voters based in small towns and suburbs tend to be more evenly distributed. As a result, Democrats are more likely to waste votes by racking up large majorities in urban districts while losing in most non-urban ones. This can allow the party with fewer votes to win legislative majorities. This problem is most visible in state legislatures, often viewed as the heart of our democracy.

America's counter majoritarian institutions have left us vulnerable to undemocratic situations in which electoral minorities prevail over majorities and are capable of transforming authoritarian minorities into governing majorities. In other words, far from checking authoritarian power, our institutions could easily augment it.

CHAPTER 15

Voters' Guide

Powers to Change America

"The people are the only legitimate fountain of power, and it is from them that the constitutional charter, under which the several branches of government hold their power, is derived".

—James Madison

American voters have busy lives with 40-hour a week jobs, family responsibilities, social activities and more. Often politics and civic responsibilities take a back seat. Many individuals feel helpless against the massive things in life like climate altering air pollution, gerrymandering of voter districts, and foreign wars. This contributes to a feeling of powerlessness and confusion. Nevertheless, every person has the power to change America for the better. It starts with whom you vote for and why. You must make your vote have meaningful power as a counterweight to the influence of dark money on our politics. We the voters are up against powerful corporate interests with unlimited funding, spending a billion dollars on a single presidential election.

These corporations do not care about you or your family as they are unemotional. Nor do they care about your social security, Medicare, voting rights, the impact on society from their pollution, poverty, women's rights, or their ecological destruction—everything the average American cares about. You must take command of your vote, as opposed to voting mindlessly because you saw a lying negative ad about a candidate.

During election cycles 100's of thousands of ads with erroneous propaganda bombard voters into submission. Trying to convince the voter that climate change is not connected to burning fossil fuel or the problem is over burdensome government regulations. Take the time to be educated about the policy differences and democratic values. Look beyond those clever slogans, fear mongering, and demonizing rhetoric. If not, you will be voting against your family's best interest and that of this nation. Your voice can be heard by the power vested with voting.

The question in voters' minds every election cycle is who and what should I be voting for? Do not vote for any politician who cannot articulate good policies that build a stronger and better America. Vote for policies that hold the corporate political power in check. Corporations are supposed to be good citizens who behave with integrity. You cannot allow corporations to control our government and our future where they create policies in their favor. The government's role is to set policies putting guard rails in place to keep corporations from wreaking havoc on our environment, the economy and taking unfair advantage of consumers. Do not fall for corporate propaganda design to convince you that government regulations will result in higher consumer prices, layoffs, be a disincentive to invest or they will have to move overseas to be competitive.

The Corporate Political Party has infiltrated our government agencies, weakening the EPA, FDA and regulatory agencies designed to protect the public. The point is you must be mindful when it comes to voting. Your vote comes down to one simple choice. Are you voting for a government of the people, by the people and for the people or not! Everything else is just voter manipulation designed to undermine your rights, a living wage, and personal freedoms. Corporations want to get rid of constraining taxation and all social services. So do not be a sucker. Do not vote based on personalities, showmanship, or authoritarian rhetoric. Today the bad actor is Trump. In another time it could be someone else. Understand that these characters are antithetical to our democratic values and our way of life.

To help you in your decision making, I have made a list high lighting public policy that will make America by, for and of the people, establishing equal rights, and protecting public health and safety as well as your personal freedoms under the law.

VOTERS GUIDE

✓ Support voting by mail and automatic voter registration nationwide.

✓ Support the National Popular Vote Interstate Compact to ensure presidential candidates win by popular vote so every vote counts equally and not based on the electoral college.

✓ Elect at every level of government individuals who believe in democracy and will defend against voter suppression laws and corporate takeover of our government.

✓ Support the John Lewis Voting Rights Advancement Act to restore and protect the right to vote for all Americans regardless of race, background, or zip code.

✓ Vote to end fossil fuel subsidies costing taxpayers $20 billion a year. Have this money distributed to taxpayers instead. Over the next five years it would total $100 billion.

✓ Make polluters pay for their externality costs, estimated to be $2.1 trillion annually through a $75 carbon tax and higher corporate tax. The carbon tax revenue can offset employee payroll tax, so consumers don't pay any part of the tax per ton of carbon. Recovered revenues can be used toward individual purchase of electric vehicles, home and businesses energy efficiency solutions to lower home energy consumption usage.

- ✓ Vote to shut down remaining coal plants and use their external cost savings of $500 billion a year for energy retrofits of homes and businesses tied to coal-derived electricity. Fund the environmental coal reclamation projects required in 17 coal production states.
- ✓ Fix the long term viability of Social Security by removing the cap rate on income earned.
- ✓ Set a new minimum tax on incomes over $400,000; individuals (25%) and corporations (28%). Increase the corporate alternative minimum tax rate from 15% to 21%.
- ✓ Vote to phase out single use plastic.
- ✓ Vote to support the $1.3 trillion 10-year farm subsidy bill that is adapting better farming and ranching practices, saving our topsoil, restoring the prairie grasslands, and shifting away from unsustainable fossil fuel dependency. Curb large corporations' access to money in the farm bill subsidies in favor of smaller American farmers while protecting our natural environment and our remaining wildlife.
- ✓ Vote for single payer universal health care to bring down costs and reduce chronic and acute diseases. No American needs to be denied healthcare or go broke paying for medical services.
- ✓ Vote for "Patients' Bill of Rights to enable consumers to make better informed decisions, thereby reducing the use of prescription drugs, avoiding unnecessary invasive procedures, reducing administrative complexity, fixing pricing failures, and receiving a coordinated scope of care delivery.
- ✓ Vote for forensic financial accounting at the Pentagon. Military spending is another area that is marred with waste, fraud, and abuse costing $50 to $80 billion of its budget. The solution is to cut the Pentagon budget by $80 billion, and make it the

Pentagon's responsibility to go after those dollars. Any contract supplier, parts supplier and or manufacturer who cheats the American taxpayer should face financial restitution and serve mandatory prison time to eliminate or discourage future fraud in the system.

- ✓ Vote to reign in the CIA's forging clandestine activities, holding it accountable through a special Congressional intelligence committee.

- ✓ Vote to establish a new foreign policy incentive to reduce U.S. military interventions and increase peace maker policies. Congress should allocate 10% of the pentagon budget to seed a peace agency that endeavors to create peace initiatives with adversaries and define ways to prevent military conflict around the globe where nations have incentives for collaboration and coexistence.

- ✓ Vote for a tougher Corporate Crime Enforcement and Penalties Act. Congress needs to provide the financial resources for the justice department to go after illegal corporate activities. Those companies that are convicted must be prevented from receiving any government contracts. CEOs should be held accountable for their crimes including jail.

- ✓ Vote for legislation requiring chemical companies to prove their products won't harm people or the environment. There are over 80,000 chemicals in our environment creating toxic cocktails of all sorts. These chemicals are in your home, in your yard, in your cosmetics, in our dog food and in the food your family eats. Europe has a new proposal to remove 12,000 toxic chemicals to lower the chemical intensity in their schools, homes, and businesses. Since the research is already done, tell your politicians to pass legislation to ban these same 12,000 toxic chemicals. Removing these harmful chemicals from society will reduce human illnesses caused by the toxic environment in which we live.

✓ Vote to replace "factory farms" on which large numbers of livestock are raised indoors in conditions intended to maximize production at minimal cost. Factory farms consume 75% of all antibiotics used in America and breed the most dangerous pathogens possible, releasing deadly gases such as sulfide, ammonia, methyl mercaptan, methyl sulfides, particulate matter, and airborne animal allergens that cause a range of illnesses, including severe respiratory problems, gastrointestinal diseases, eye infections, nosebleeds, nausea, miscarriage, and physiological problems. Such emissions are illegal.

✓ Vote for the Raise the Wage Act to increase the federal minimum wage to $15. The Congressional Budget Office estimated that the bill would boost the pay of twenty-seven million American workers and lift 1.3 million households out of poverty. In a Hill Harris poll of registered voters, 81% expressed support for the minimum wage increase but the minority-controlled Senate killed the Wage Act because of corporate political influence. So, talk to your senators and tell them to pass the minimum Wage Act. States with minimum wage at $7.25 are Alabama, Georgia, Idaho, Indiana, Iowa, Kansas, Kentucky, Louisiana, Mississippi, North Carolina, North Dakota, New Hampshire, Oklahoma, South Carolina, Tennessee, Texas, Utah, Wisconsin, West Virginia, and Wyoming. Not surprisingly these states have the highest poverty rates.

✓ Vote for gun control. Since 2020 over six hundred mass shootings have taken place every year, generating broad public support for stricter gun laws. Surveys by Gallup and Pew have consistently found more than 60% support laws banning the manufacture, sale, or possession of semi-automatic or assault weapons, and more than 80% support laws requiring universal background checks for gun purchases. Unless voters demand action on common sense gun reform the Senate will remain the graveyard of gun control legislation and innocent children and the public at large will continue to be gunned down by weapons of war shredding bodies into pieces.

✓ Vote for the Anti-Corruption and Public Integrity Act and the Corporate Capture Act to stop the undue influence by corporate lobbyists writing and implementing legislation.

✓ Vote for the "Freedom to Vote Act."

✓ Vote for the "Save Oak Flat Act."

✓ Vote for "End Polluter Welfare Act" of 2020.

✓ Vote for "Fracking Ban Act."

✓ Vote for "College for All Act."

✓ Vote for "Medicare for All Act."

✓ Vote for "Prescription Drug Price Relief Act."

✓ Vote for the Border Bill-immigration funding and policy provisions in the "Emergency National Security Supplemental Appropriations Act."

✓ Vote for women's reproductive rights. The Supreme Court's 2022 decision in Dobbs V Jackson eliminated the constitutionally protected rights to an abortion. According to the Pew Research Center, 61% of US adults say abortion should be legal in all or most cases, while only 37% believe abortion should be illegal in all or most cases.

✓ Vote for the "Supreme Court Ethics and Investigations Act", the Supreme Court Ethics, Recusal, and Transparency

(SCERT) Act and the Judicial Ethics and Anti-Corruption Act to formally establish a code of conduct for Supreme Court Justices.

Voters often wonder if the economy does better under Democratic or Republican presidents. A report by Alan S. Blinder and Mark W. Watson, economists at Princeton University, indicates the economy has performed much better during democratic administrations. Economic growth, job creation, stock market returns, and industrial production have all been stronger under democrats. Ten of the last eleven recessions have occurred under Republican administrations.

According to the www.PresidentialData.org. since 1961, GDP has grown 44% higher, business investments have been 132% higher, and 43.8 million more jobs have been created all under Democrat Presidents, whereas the trade deficit has been 15% higher, budget deficits 9% higher, unemployment 5% higher and Federal Spending 221% higher under Republican Presidents.

CHAPTER 16

Mr. Smith Goes to Washington

"Let us not seek the republican answer or the democratic answer, but the right answer. Let us not seek to fix the blame for the past. Let us accept our own responsibility for the future."

—John F. Kennedy

By way of illustration of whom you should vote for; imagine for a moment that Mr. Smith comes to Washington. He announces his candidacy for President of the United States, and gives a televised speech on the steps of the capital addressing all Americans. The speech is a shining example of what you should hear and look for from future presidential candidates.

Mr. Smiths' Speech!

Fellow citizens of this great nation.

Today, I stand before you not just as a candidate, but a citizen deeply concerned about the direction of our nation and the state of the world. Even in the face of these challenges, I am filled with hope, hope for a future where every individual can thrive, regardless of his or her background or circumstances, hope for a world where our planet is cherished and protected for generations to come, hope for a society where every person's rights are respected and upheld. Everyone must come together as patriotic Americans, recognize our shared values and relate to one another with dignity, respect and civility. Together we can restore our democratic norms as no nation can afford to abandon its founding principles, moral authority, and highest ideals. Today we face overwhelming challenges: Extensive pollution of our air and water, and soil, unfair tax policies, persistent income inequality, social and judicial injustices, systemic racism, and voter suppression. Our healthcare costs are out of control. We have the homeless to house, and public education needs. Corporate agents have infiltrated the House of Representatives, US Senate, and government agencies. We must work together to solve our social media misinformation crisis, foreign tax havens, cyber security risks, cartels operating in America, gun violence, fentanyl and opioid epidemic, border security, immigration reform, factory farm contagion risks, food and water insecurity and unsustainable farming practices.

Democracy thrives when every voice is heard, and every vote is counted. We must work to dismantle barriers to voting and ensure that every eligible citizen can participate in our democratic process freely and fairly. We must defend women's reproductive rights. Every women deserves the right to make her own choices about her body and her future. We must ensure access to safe and affordable healthcare, including reproductive healthcare, for all individuals, regardless of gender. We must reevaluate Americas approach to foreign intervention. We cannot continue to engage in endless wars that only serve to destabilize regions and cost countless lives. We must prioritize diplomacy and international cooperation to address global challenges and promote peace and security.

Urgently we have an existential planetary climate crisis threatening our survival. Ecological collapse is no longer a prediction but a real and present danger that cannot be denied. Today humans are the force changing our climate. It is imperative that every American recognize the precarious reality we are living in. The level of environmental degradation by human activity is accelerating at an alarming rate. Evidence demonstrates that we have exceeded the sustainability of the planet by 25%. What does this mean? It means we exceeded the constraint of natural forces in nature that support our lives. This has been caused by human induced harmful emissions warming the planet, deforestation, and land-use changes.

Excess carbon and methane has weaponized nature, hitting us with consecutive mega storms, rain bombs, sky rivers, flash flooding, cyclone bombs, snow bursts, heat waves, heat blobs, extended droughts, and fire tornados. We have exponentially gone from 280 PPM of carbon to over 421 PPM in less than 70 years. This carbon is now trapped in the earth's atmosphere and is measurable. As such we have caused large scale planetary shifts in our natural environment, including more than a 2% oxygen level deficit in the air we breathe, the melting of Arctic Sea ice, changing jet streams and ocean current patterns as well as seasonal weather, creating heat waves in Siberia destabilizing methane hydrates, increasing ocean acidity causing fish to struggle to survive. Sulfuric acid droplets are in our atmosphere and our cities are polluted with toxic molecules. Since 2008 three hundred seventy six million climate refugees were forcibly on the move, eating powdered meals to survive. Underscoring what is to come. Scientist estimates that by 2050 there will be 1.2 billion climate refugees.

Across the world massive forest fires have destroyed vast wilderness areas and caused the death of countless wildlife. Recently massive flash flooding has taken place on every continent causing death, destruction, and homelessness. Twenty thousand cold snap records and forty thousand hot temperature records have been broken. In 2024, the world exceeded the safe level of 1.5 degree Celsius, recommended by the Intergovernmental Panel on Climate Change, reaching 2 degrees Celsius above safe levels. In just 7 years from now it is estimated we will hit 2.7 degrees Celsius above safe levels. Remember, half of all CO2 emissions have been emitted in just the last thirty years. We are on an exponential curve accelerating the impact of carbon and methane pollution on the planet. We must act to avoid abrupt changes with no ability to fix the problem, leaving us with a hot uninhabitable planet.

We as a nation have had a flaw in our thinking continued from one generation to the next. That is the false premise of extracting eco systems for profits. It is this kind of thinking which has led us to our current predicament of collapsing fragile ecosystems, when the highest productive values come from preserving eco systems as a source of abundance and regeneration. It is time to restore our biological life forms for our own survival's sake, ensuring our planet is recognizable and inhabitable in the coming decades. Man induced climate change can only be fixed by retooling our society with options that do not destroy our natural environment while sustaining our lives. Solving these problems will involve every citizen, legislature, corporation, financial market, small business, and government agency. It will affect job options, what we buy, how we source and use energy and how we treat one another.

A clean more prosperous economy requires correcting current market failures, in which polluters profit from environmental damage while losses are effectively being subsidized by society at large. Most Americans understand it is unfair for industry to pass on environmental degradation and healthcare costs to taxpayers. Burning fossil fuel is the smoking gun. It threatens our way of life, and its societal costs are no longer bearable. It is dangerous, deadly, and finite. Air pollution kills over 8.3 million people a year world-wide and according to the American Lung Association, over 40% of the U.S. population, 134 million people are at risk of premature death because of chemical air pollution. In the United States the annual societal costs from burning fossil fuels, including healthcare costs, environmental degradation and subsidies exceeds $2.1 trillion annually. Globally that cost is over $8.1 trillion.

As your president, I will declare a planetary climate crisis emergency to protect our national security and the American way of life. It is now too late for any half measures. It requires putting an end to the fossil fuel era altogether. To become good stewards of the planet we must reduce half of our carbon emissions by 2030 and be 100% carbon neutral by 2050. The US will immediately begin an orderly shutdown of exiting coal plants, and transform our current transportation system to an all-electric one, thereby, ending the manufacturing of the internal combustion automobile. Consumers will get cash rebates and tax credits as incentives to buy electric vehicles. The US government will purchase electric vehicles for its own use and provide incentives for states and counties to go electric. Our electric transportation system will be supported with the installation of 500,000 electric charging stations across America and an electric charging station in every garage. The U.S. will capture market share from the sale of electric cars, trucks, buses, solar and wind power plants, biomass, geothermal, hydrogen fuels and power plants with zero emissions.

Over the past century the United States has lost 150 million acres of wildlife habitat and farmland to development. Along the Louisiana Coast 2,000 square miles of wetland have been lost to oil and gas development. Since the 1970's across North America we have lost over three billion birds. I will support habitat restoration wherever and whenever possible to protect and increase wildlife numbers. A focus of my administration will be to preserve our biodiversity by protecting wildlife areas from extraction industries. I will do what I can to stop the Arctic Willow project in Alaska and will protect Alaska's magnificent Bristol Bay wilderness from Northern Dynasty Minerals' Pebble Beach mining project. A fully developed Pebble Mine would create ten billion tons of waste mining debris, leaving a gargantuan open pit mine two miles deep and wide enough to hold the Empire State building. It would have a catastrophic impact on wildlife, local fisheries, and the livelihood of 15,000 local inhabitants.

I will support the removal of the Winchester Dam in Oregon and the Electron Dam in Washington to allow salmon species to survive and thrive. I will take steps to protect Lake Koocanusa from selenium pollution from coal mining along the Montana and Canadian border. I will stop the industrial waste pipeline from cutting through the Iroquois National Wildlife Refuge. I will work to stop the Canadian oil giant Enbridge's Line 5 pipeline that threatens the Great Lakes areas. I will end the manufacturing of lead ammunitions in America. I will require FEMA money to rebuild Puerto Rico's energy system to be self-sufficient with solar and wind with battery storage.

I will push for a national Renewable Portfolio Standard (RPS) based on each state's renewable energy resource potential. State and federal agencies will work together with industry to build 100,000 megawatts of wind turbines, solar arrays and zero emissions power generation plants. My administration will work with the Federal Energy Regulatory Agency (FERC) to build and improve the smart grid to transport the new megawatts of renewable power generation. We will establish new investment tax credits for all renewable energy technology solutions. Furthermore, investments will be made into science and technology research and development to make sure the US leads the world in the carbon free technology of the future. Commercial airplane fleets will transition to hybrid electric clean jet fuels. Manufacturers will adapt cradle to grave consumer products moving beyond our throw away practices. American farmers will shift to no till soil regenerative farming methods. We will plant millions of trees across America and participate in worldwide tree planting initiatives.

To protect Americans from harmful chemicals the EPA must enforce our clean air and water laws. The EPA must end any exemptions under the Clean Air and Water Act. The EPA will identify and end chemical contaminants going into our air, food, water, and soil. I will call on Congress to ban harmful food additives and thousands of other chemicals studies have deemed harmful to humans. We must make every effort possible to reduce autism, neurological disorders, liver disease, infertility, Parkinson's, Alzheimer's, cognitive learning disorders and other forms of cancer afflicting society, as well as those chemicals destroying bee populations.

All fossil fuel power generation plants and pipelines will be assessed for methane leaks. Worldwide there are twenty-nine million orphaned oil and gas wells emitting 2.5 million tons of methane per year. In the US that number is 3.2 million abandoned oil and gas wells emitting 281 kilotons of methane. Methane gas is a twenty-eight times more potent greenhouse gas than carbon. We must work with industry owners and states to get these leaking wells capped. It will require 250,000 workers to complete this task over the next four years. Additional measures will include prosecution for illegal activities, ending all fossil fuel subsidies and stopping the issuance of new permits or licenses for oil and gas exploration. My administration will work to claw back on sweetheart resource extraction deals, require restitution payment for environmental degradation impacts and for workers cheated out of their pension funds.

To borrow from John F Kennedy's moon-shot speech: "We choose to do this societal energy transformation and other things in this decade not because they are easy but because they are hard and something we must do. Because this goal will serve to organize and measure the best of our energies and skills, because that challenge is one that we are willing to accept, one we are no longer willing to postpone, and one which we intend to win, and the others, too." The foundation of our civilization is based on a stable climate. I call upon a deep love of country and patriotism to mobilize all Americans on this audacious mission to decarbonize our society. This "Clean Energy Ecological Mission" will be the most wise and profound transformation the world has ever known.

In lock step with Congress, we will develop the legislative framework, I have named HSB 2024 "The Clean Energy Ecological Industrial Act." Together we will turn on the greatest economic engine in the world. Unleashing American ingenuity, technological innovation, hard work, and grit to decarbonize our society as a model for the rest of the world. Let there be no doubt! No doubt at all! We know how to mitigate our planetary climate crisis. We know how to transform our agricultural farming methods to regenerative soil practices to absorb a third of our carbon emissions. We know how to cut energy consumption by a third through energy efficiency and how to complete the electrification of our transportation system, as well as transforming the energy sector to renewable energy power generation and clean fuels.

The tools of capitalism will be unbridled to build a more prosperous, equitable and stable clean economy. A mass mobilization of capital will fund earth restoration works and carbon sequestration as we transition to a clean economy. The clean energy economy is worth over $27 trillion dollars in new Gross Domestic Product (GDP) growth. For every 1% in GDP growth, the economy gains $1 trillion dollars over a ten-year period. The economics favor the less expensive renewable energy technologies, avoiding externality costs and environmental calamity, providing better public health for the American family.

It is important not to lose sight of the long-term future need for food and water security. Our current methods of farming are not sustainable. Water supplies and our farmland yields are in decline. Alarmingly, 40% of bees have died from toxic chemicals. One out of every three bites of food we eat depends on these bee pollinators. Topsoil loss, higher temperatures, and the neutering of biological life forms in our soils from chemical farming methods are unsustainable. We have fewer than sixty growing seasons left on our farmlands. The good news is we can reverse this trend by shifting to proven organic soil regenerative farming methods to grow healthy food while sequestering carbon. The new $1.3 trillion ten-year farm bill is loaded with innovative farming practices that are moving America farmers and ranchers in the right direction. Shifting to proven organic farming methods uses less water, and soil regeneration practices can be free from harmful herbicides and pesticides, while producing higher crop yields, enabling the public to have access to food and water without chemical contamination.

We have no time to waste in quarrelsome partisanship while the nation is suffering, and delays only make matters worse. Let us cooperatively work together rebuilding our nation to its greatest potential. Our mutual long-term economic health and our national security are in everyone's best interests. Change can be hard and sometimes downright painful but together we can build back this nation better. We must think about the livability of the planet today for our children and grandchildren's sake. After all, the earth is the only habitable planet in our solar system, and we are human inhabitants of the same species. Together, we can ensure that America remains a beacon of hope, opportunity, and progress for the world.

I have traveled across America visiting red and blue states. The experience was like visiting two vastly different countries with two vastly different economies. What I discovered and since verified was red states had the poorest health, were least educated, received the lowest pay, had highest rate of obesity, highest crime rates, highest drug use, most alcohol-related auto accidents, highest homicide rates and a welfare dependency receiving the greatest amount of Federal dollars. Red state murder rates were 33% higher than blue states in both 2021 and 2022. Murder rates in the twenty-five states Trump won in 2020 are 40% greater than in the states Biden won. Cumulative COVID 19 death rates in red states was 30% higher than blue states. Blue counties generate 79% of the US GNP whereas red counties produce only 21% of the US GNP. If you live in a red state your world view would be quite different, a world view based on witnessing more crime, higher amounts of drug abuse, poor health, higher food prices, stagnant wages, and a lack of upward mobility. Someone living in a red state would conclude that life's not so good, and things are moving in the wrong direction.

The Republican House majority has failed to pass the Raise the Wage Act to increased minimum hourly wage from $7.25 to $17.00 per hour by 2028, raising 19% of the workforce or 27,855 million workers out of poverty with an annual pay increase of $3,100. Republican attitudes about raising the minimum wage are telling. For example, Virginia Governor Glenn Youngkin vetoed a wage increase to $15.00. Former governor Bush said wage increases should be left to the private sector. Republican Senator Marco Rubio, earning an annual salary of $170,000 with a net worth of $85 million, forcibly objected to a minimum wage increase from $7.25 per hour, claiming that workers would cost more than machines. Republicans have cut funding for healthcare services, blocked Medicaid expansion, cut funding to education, housing assistance, job training, supplemental nutrition assistance, cut summer food assistance for eight million children in 2024, cut childcare assistance, public transit, and law enforcement services.

What has caused such disparity between red and blue states in America? And what can be done to fix this crisis in red states? It is enlightening to know that the cause and the fix is the same. Republican state legislators, House Representatives and Senators have failed the citizens living in red states. If you are living in a red state, your elected republican officials have failed to meet your community and family needs. Their corporate backers are enriching themselves at your expense. If you want the same benefits and quality of life as your counterparts in blue states such as a living wage, quality education, health benefits, reduced crime & drug use, an environment free from high pollution levels, safe drinking water, access to fresh fruits and vegetables and so much more, then you must vote out of office every republican representative who has failed to advocate for your rights, ensuring you a better quality of life.

In addition to our climate crisis, and standard of living in red states, we have a democracy crisis facing the nation. We have a demagogue Donald Trump running for a second term and the 50-year-old conservative Heritage Foundation ready to implement their project 2025 plan. This comprehensive plan is to take power over America at 12 noon on January 25th, 2025. This group has published a 920-page manifesto blueprint to put a conservative executive in the White House with extended presidential powers answering to no one, severing shared power within the three branches of government and thereby destroying our functioning democracy and seizing the reins of power over the U.S. government. The plan is to gut all government agencies in the name of the constitutional rights and good white Christian family values. An army of 20,000 weaponized likeminded trained conservatives will be ready to do battle against the federal government. The project's goal is to rescue the country from the grip of the radical left, uniting the conservative movement against elite rule and woke culture.

Conservative extremists believe the federal government is weaponized against American citizens and conservative values, and that freedoms, and personal liberties are under siege as never before. The 2025 project's task is to reverse this trend and restore the Republic to its original moorings, returning to self-governance. The group is anti-globalist, anti-environmentalist, anti LGBTQ+, anti-women's rights, anti-democracy with a Christian nationalist agenda at every level of government. Federal employees whose positions have been determined to be of a confidential policy nature, and determining policymaking, or policy advocating character will be replaced under Schedule F of the Civil Service Reform Act of 1978. Supporters of Schedule F propose converting 50,000 career civil servants into political appointee status. Essentially creating a partisan politicization centered around political loyalty to the president. The President with unchecked power will be able to fire at will, gut environmental protection laws in favor of polluting industries and take away individual freedoms. We must not allow the Heritage Foundation, Koch Industries, and the Corporate Political Party to destroy our democracy and dictate the future of America.

We are all bound together in the same web of life. We are being summoned to rise to an occasion to fulfill a civic duty. We all have a responsibility to overcome our differences for the sake of this nation and the American family. The gap between what is and what could be has never been greater in all of history. As your President, I will chart a course to transform the nation from one of divisiveness & fear to one of unity and collaboration. I will protect the government of, for and by the people, maintain presidential norms and defend everyone's constitutional rights. I will lead America's transition from a destructive carbon-based economy to a non-inflationary, clean energy more resilient one, an economy that works within the limits of our natural environment with no one left out—no one left out of a job, housing, a living wage, education, public safety, or affordable health care. This will be a society of equal justice under the law and a society steeped in preparedness for any future viruses and disease, increasing the American family's peace of mind, dignity, and financial stability in a safe, clean environment in which to live.

Thank you. I wish the absolute best for all Americans.

CHAPTER 17

Glossary of Terms

"Many forms of government have been tried and will be tried in this world of sin and woe. No one pretends that democracy is perfect or all wise. Indeed, it has been said, that democracy is the worst form of government except for all those other forms that have been tried from time to time."

—Winston Churchill

Americans for Prosperity

Americans for Prosperity was founded in 2004 as a libertarian conservative political advocacy group in the United States, affiliated with brothers Charles Koch and the late David Koch. The AFP is an organization of grassroots leaders who engage citizens in the name of limited government and free markets on local, state, and federal levels. The grassroots activists of AFP advocate for public policies that champion their principles of entrepreneurship and fiscal and regulatory restraint.

Authoritarianism

Is a government ruled by a dictator whereby personal freedoms are subordinated to the strict obedience to authority and there is a complete disregard for the opinions and wishes of others.

Autocratic rule

Autocracy is a system of government in which absolute power over a state is concentrated in the hands of one person, whose decisions are subject neither to external legal constraints nor to regularized mechanisms of popular control.

Cato Institute

The Cato Institute is an American libertarian think tank headquartered in Washington, DC. It was founded in 1977 by Ed Crane, Murray Rothbard, and Charles Koch, Chairperson and chief executive officer of Koch Industries. The mission of the Cato Institute is the increased understanding of public policies based on principles of limited government, free markets, individual liberty, and peace.

Centrist

A centrist is someone having moderate views on policy, who supports the center of a range of political opinions. A Centrist goes against both left-and right-wing politics. The label is used for political parties, organizations and groups that believe in centrism.

Christian Fundamentalism

Christian Fundamentalism is a conservative protestant movement of people who adhere to a literal interpretation of the Bible that enacts a strict code of conduct for its church members. Christian fundamentalists believe that the bibles without error or fault in all of it teachings and will accomplish exactly what God wants. They believe in the virgin birth of Christ and that Christ's death was an atonement for sin. They believe in the bodily resurrection of Christ and the historical reality of all Christ's miracles. They believe that God created the world in a single week and that everything was made perfectly at the time. They totally reject the Theory of Evolution.

Communism

Communism is based on the teachings of Karl Marx's idea of government and an economic system to create and share wealth. In a communist system, individuals do not own land, factories, or machinery. Instead, the government or the whole community owns these things. Everyone is supposed to share the wealth that they create. In a communist society there is no private property or social classes. Communist party rule is totalitarian in nature and oppressive against any political dissent. It is often associated with ethnic cleansing, forced collectivization, religious persecution and uses forced labor in concentration camps. No communist can become a US citizen.

Conservatism

Conservatism is an aesthetic, cultural, social, and political philosophy, which promotes and preserves traditional social institutions. Core principles are individual freedoms, limited government, rule of law, peace through strength, fiscal responsibility, free markets, and human dignity.

Constitutional Republic:

Limit power to the people on the premise that the business class is better suited in deciding prominent issues for the country as opposed to ordinary citizens. The real intention of the constitution was never intended to have a majority rule. Let the business elite decide.

Corporate Capture

Corporate capture is a phenomenon where private industry uses its political influence to take control of the decision-making apparatus of the state.

Corporate Political Party (CPP)

The Corporate Political Party is made up of the corporate elites, rich powerful companies and conservative think tanks who exert pressure on the U.S. government on behalf of business interests.

Dark Money

Funds raised for the purpose of influencing elections by nonprofit organizations that are not required to disclose the identities of their donors. In 2010, in the landmark case *Citizens United versus Federal Election Commission (FEC)*, the Supreme Court held that independent expenditures, including those made by corporations, do not give rise to corruption or the appearance of corruption. Unlike Super PACS organizations who are required by law to disclose donors' names, these Dark money nonprofits are not. Proponents of dark money maintain it is protected under the Fifth Amendment as free speech. Critics complain recipients of dark money are beholden to their funders. Therefore, voters are kept in the dark about connections between donors and politicians when favors are paid back.

As of 2022, the nonprofit OpenSecrets states that dark money is "pouring" into US elections, but not only are its donors not being disclosed, the total quantity of dark money is not either. "The vast majority" of what is spent "is not being disclosed to the Federal Election Commission." In 2020 election cycle, there was more than $1 billion in undisclosed dark money spending. Dark money donors want to avoid ridicule and blowback from voters for the things they support.

Democracy

A democracy is a form of government in which all eligible citizens have the right to participate equally either directly or through elected representatives in the creation of law.

Democratic Party

Founded in 1828 it is the oldest active political party in the world. The old democratic party was racist and supported slavery to maintain their economic interests, which led to the Civil War of 1862. Today the Democratic party seeks to promote social programs, labor unions, consumer protection, workplace safety regulations, equal opportunity, disability rights, racial equity, women s rights, LGBTQ+ rights, rights to healthcare, access to education, fair taxation, personal freedoms, regulations to curb pollution altering climate change, regenerative farming practices, reforestation, and criminal justice reform.

Donors Trust

Donors Trust is an American nonprofit founded in 1999 with the goal of safeguarding the intent of libertarian and conservative donors. As a donor Advised Fund, Donors Trust is not legally required to disclose the identity of its owners, so its donors remain anonymous. It distributes funds to various conservative and libertarian organizations and has been characterized as "the dark money ATM" of the political right.

Externality Costs

External costs are costs that are not borne by the person or entity that causes them. They are often the result of market failures, such as when the company pollutes the environment without paying for the cleanup costs. One real world example of an external cost is pollution. If a firm were paying the full cost of production, it would return clean air to the atmosphere. Instead, if society wants clean air, society must pay to clean it. So, in this case pollution represents the shifting of the costs of production to society, which has a negative impact. It is an indirect cost that decreases the quality of life and increases health care costs. Externalities can be considered unpriced goods involved in either consumer's or producer's market transactions. Pollution is considered an externality cost not reflected in the pricing of the commodity, which has caused pollution. These economic costs are real such as disability from chronic disease $200 billion, asthma $17 billion, preterm births $90 billion, sick leave $100 billion, child deaths $50 billion, adult deaths $2.4 billion. Total costs are estimated at $2.1 trillion or 3.3% of global GDP. Health care costs alone are $820 billion annually. Pollution has been termed an externality because it imposes costs on people who are external to the producer.

Fascism

Fascism is a far-right form of government in which most of the country's power is held by one ruler or a small group, under a single party. Fascist governments are usually totalitarian and authoritarian one-party states. The most notorious examples are Benito Mussolini's National Fascist Party in Italy from 1922 to 1943 and Adolf Hitler's National Socialist German Workers Party, the Nazi Party from 1933 to 1945. Fascism is based on an ethnic division between us and them, and nostalgia for a mystic past, typically in which members of a chosen ethnic group had an empire.

Federalist Society

The Federalist Society Law and Public Policy Studies is an American conservative and libertarian legal organization that advocates for a textualist and originalist interpretation of the US Constitution.

Fiscal Conservatives

Fiscal conservatives advocate for tax cuts, reduced government spending. free markets, deregulation, privatization, free trade, and minimal government debt. Fiscal conservatism follows the same philosophical outlook as classical liberalism. This concept is derived from economic liberalism.

Fossil Fuel

Fossil fuel is a generic term for non-renewable energy sources such as coal, coal products, natural gas derived gas, crude oil, and petroleum products. These fuels originate from plants and animals that existed in the geological past millions of years ago. Fossil fuels can also be made from industrial processes from other fossil fuels. In the oil refinery process crude oil is transformed into gasoline. Fossil fuels are carbon based and their combustion results in the release of carbon into the Earth's atmosphere. It is estimated 74% of all human-caused CO2 and greenhouse gas emissions originate from fossil fuel combustion.

Fusion Presidency

Fusion Presidency is when a president supports corporate interests over public interests and actively works on their behalf to ensure unfettered access to American resources and tax favors without cumbersome, annoying, and costly regulations. Examples of presidents who engaged in corporate fusion include Ronald Reagan, George Walker Bush, Bill Clinton, George W. Bush and most recently Donald Trump.

GOP

In the 1870's republicans began to adapt the GOP acronym which stood for "Grand Old Party." From then on, the Republican party has been referred to by the nickname GOP.

Heritage Foundation

The fifty plus year old Heritage Foundation stands for free enterprise, limited government, individual freedom, traditional American values, and a strong National Defense. They object to such policies as the Green New Deal (transitioning to a clean economy) and Medicare for all. An activist American conservative think tank based in Washington, DC Founded in 1973, the Heritage Foundation took a leading role in the conservative movement in the 1980s during the presidency of Ronald Reagan, and has historically been ranked among the most important or influential public policy organizations in the United States. The Heritage Foundation is an associate member of the State Policy Network, founded in 1992, a network of conservative and libertarian organizations financed by the Koch brothers, Philip Morris, and other corporate sources.

Independent

An independent voter is a non-affiliated voter in the United States, a voter who does not align with any political party.

Laissez-faire

An idea that government needs to get out of the way of American business and let the free capital market due its thing. It has historically been proven repeatedly that market economies need regulatory oversight. Otherwise greed will take over, pushing economies to collapse and environmental degradation to unlivable conditions.

Liberal

Liberals believe a wide array of views depending on their understanding of these principles, but in general support individual, civil, and human rights, democracy, secularism, freedom of speech, freedom of press, freedom of religion, and a market economy.

Libertarianism

Libertarians believe the government should have less control over people's lives. Libertarianism primarily seeks to reduce power of the state to safeguard individualism. The Libertarian Party Platform has campaigned to abolish government agencies and repeal all taxation.

Minority Rule

Minority rule occurs when a political party controls most political structures and decision making but receives less than 50% of the votes in an election.

Majority Rule

The majority rule is the principle that the group that is supported by more than half of all voters should be allowed to make the decisions. The majority rule is most often used in decision-making bodies, including legislatures of democratic nations.

Majoritarian

The concept of a majoritarian electoral system usually gives a majority of the seats to the party with a plurality of votes. Majoritarianism is often referred to as majority rule.

Narcissist

A narcissist has a personality disorder that is characterized by a feeling of entitlement, a high sense of self-importance, arrogance, a need for admiration, and a lack of empathy.

Oligarchy

An oligarchy is a government by the few in which rulers are selected from a small class of elites and often despotic power is exercised by a small and privileged group for corrupt or selfish purposes.

Powell Memo

The Lewis Powell Memo, written in 1971, offered a blueprint for the rise of the American conservative movement and the formation of a network of influential right-wing think tanks and lobbying organizations to dominate American democracy.

Progressive

In politics the progressive movement believes in the advancement of our human condition through social reforms, science, and technology. Progressives think government should have an active role in improving our overall society. Progressives want universal health care, the ability to earn a living wage, to end poverty and income inequality, progressive taxation, the advancement of justice and peace and the right of every American to retire with security and dignity.

Q-Anon Conspiracy

The Q-Anon conspiracy theory a platform that profits by peddling various conspiracy theories, secret plans to do something that is unlawful and or harmful to others. Q-Anon followers have disrupted business, defamed celebrities, committed murder and participated in the January 6 insurrection.

According to recent poll by the Public Religion Research Institute (PRRI) a quarter of republicans and one in four Evangelicals believe in the baseless claims of Q-Anon.

Religious Right

The religious right is a political movement, prominent since the 1970s, that advocates social and political conservatism. Its agenda often includes attempts to restore prayer in public schools, to invalidate abortion on demand, and to prohibit state recognition of same-sex marriage. Although these issues often appeal to fundamentalists of other religions, most of the recent leaders of this movement have been evangelical Christians.

Renewable Energy Technologies

Renewable energy is energy that comes from sources that will not run out, such as wind, solar, bioenergy, geothermal and tidal energy. These are all energy sources that are self-replenishing and therefore, non-inflationary sources of energy that do not have any climate altering pollution as an external cost. Renewable energy sources are less expensive than fossil fuels and are better for the environment.

Republican Party

One of the two major political parties in the united States, the Republican Party was formed in 1860 in opposition to the extension of slavery to the country's new territories and, ultimately, in favor of slavery's complete abolition. During the 20th and 21st centuries the party has come to be associated laissez-faire capitalism, low taxes, and conservative social policies.

Socialism

Socialism is a social and economic doctrine that calls for public rather than private ownership or control of property and natural resources. In socialism, everything that is produced together is considered a social product so anyone who was involved in the production is entitled to share in it. Socialism is based on the idea that society should own or at least control any property for the benefit of all its members.

Staunch Conservative

A staunch conservative is someone who supports the status quo and is opposed to any social, political, or economic change. It's someone who believes that the elites in business who can understand markets know what policies are best for the country.

White Christian Nationalists

White Christian Nationalists believe that the United States was founded as a Christian nation and has been ordained so by God, that white people got here first and therefore deserve rights that other people, especially nonwhite immigrants don't, that it is their divine right and duty to fight as Jesus did in the Book of Revelation, alternately battling in a bloody holy war against the treacherous forces of the antichrist to take back the United States.

White Supremacy

White supremacy is the ideology that white people are inherently genetically superior to other races and that white people should have control over people of other races socially, economically, and in our political system. White supremacy embodies a racist hatred for other races who are considered inferior. The white supremacy movement historically included the Ku Klux Klan (KKK) and Aryan Nations. Today it includes white nationalism, white separatism, neo-Nazism, Christian identity, and white separatist movements.

Conclusion

All Americans should understand that they possess three effective personal powers often squandered, misunderstood, or taken for granted, which, used with the right awareness and collective intent can wield tremendous power and influence. Knowledge is a power that can turn the tide against any autocratic, fascist, oligarchy, or monied corporate dominance over our democracy. Voting is a power and a civic duty to ensure our personal freedoms are protected. Voting has a very profound impact on our society as elections have consequences. Each person must be clear minded about the results you want to see happen and why. You may be among the thousands of minority voters being blocked from voting, or feel that your vote will not count or will not have influence.

Do not despair. Get yourself to the polls or if you are lucky vote by mail.

Your wallet has power. How you spend your money can alter society, so, you must spend wisely and consciously, whether donating to a political campaign or investing in socially responsible companies. When buying consumer goods, be a smart shopper. Read labels to avoid toxins and processed foods and do not buy products from unethical companies. Your kitchen fork has power. Let food be your medicine. Eat right to stay healthy. The right choices dictate good personal health outcomes, the state of our farmlands and the health of our planet, and can save taxpayers over $2 trillion a year from funding a disease based healthcare system system.

There is a tug of war between people's rights and corporate political ambitions, between democracy and autocratic rule. If you want to improve your quality of life, protect individual rights and personal freedoms, you must vote out of office all deceitful political leaders.

Acknowledgments

Thank you, Arnold Schwarzenegger, for the phrase "Climate Alerting Pollution" relating to the damage being done by fossil fuels. And many thanks to Al Gore for his "Global Climate Reality Project" for inspiration. And thank you Donald Trump for exposing the magnitude of prejudice, hate and fear in American society today. The light of day will enable the healing process to begin and the divisiveness to end.

About the Author

David J. Slawson is a seasoned political analyst and advocate for informed voting. Holding a Bachelors of Science degree in Political Science from Portland State University, he has a background that spans education, healthcare, and renewable energy. As the founder of the East West College of the Healing Arts, Everett Healing Center, and the Laurelhurst Clinic, David has demonstrated a commitment to improving lives. His leadership roles as Chairman & CEO of Stirling Energy Systems and Senior Vice President at Great Ocean New Energy Development Company (GOE) in Dalian, China, highlights his expertise in sustainable development. David resides in Oregon with his family.

Made in the USA
Middletown, DE
28 July 2024

58039532R00135